A SURVEY OF THE WOMAN PROBLEM

A SURVEY OF THE WOMAN PROBLEM

FROM THE GERMAN OF
ROSA MAYREDER

BY HERMAN SCHEFFAUER

HYPERION PRESS, INC.
Westport, Connecticut

Published in 1913 by G.H. Doran Company, New York
Hyperion reprint edition 1983,1994
Library of Congress Catalog Number 79-2944
ISBN 0-8305-0108-8
Printed in the United States of America

Library of Congress Cataloging in Publication Data

Mayreder, Rosa Obermayer, 1858-1938.
  A survey of the woman problem.

    Translation of: Zur Kritik der Weiblichkeit.
    Reprint. Originally published: New York :
G. H. Doran Co., 1913.
    1. Feminism—Addresses, essays, lectures. 2. Women
—Addresses, essays, lectures. I. Title.
HQ1210.M313 1983   305.4'2   79-2944
ISBN 0-8305-0108-8   AACR2

PREFACE

In this book I have dealt in my own way with the problems of the woman's movement. Although in some respects I am not in entire agreement with this movement, I regard it, nevertheless, as one of the phenomena which honourably distinguish the present epoch from all previous periods of human history; nay, more, it seems to me to be one of the finest manifestations of an epoch which otherwise, in its poverty of ideals, of noble feelings, and of passionate beliefs, betrays evidence of degeneration.

Many of the ideas contained in my work may frequently have been expressed before. The first outlines were made fifteen years ago, and certain experiences of my early youth gave me the initial impulse to write it. Those readers, however, who are already acquainted with the literature on the subject will, I hope, find enough that is new to compensate them for what is old; while that large majority which, unfortunately, still knows very little about the movement, must remain satisfied with the comprehensive view of it which I have endeavoured to present. Some of the essays have already appeared in various periodicals, and in stringing them together it has been impossible to avoid repeti-

tions.   These will not vex the reader who recognises
that certain truths cannot be repeated too often, since
that which stands to reason does not necessarily compel
belief, and that which is proved is not always admitted.

The woman's movement is due to three different
causes, and has three different aims in view.   In my
opinion, these ought to be considered separately, however intimately they may be connected with one another,
and however true it may be that, taken in conjunction
with one another, they constitute the essential movement.   Its threefold basis is economic, social, ethical-
psychological.

During the few years in which the movement has
begun to pass from the theoretical stage to the political,
the economic and social problems have come to the front,
while the ethical-psychological part has been kept in the
background.   I have, however, not dealt at all with the
economic, and only slightly with the social, sides of the
question.   Although I recognise that without the
economic revolution caused by the introduction of
machinery the movement could hardly have become a
practical one, yet I maintain that historically it has an
idealistic, not a materialistic, origin.   However great
an influence the economic impulses may exert, much
more importance is to be attached to the ideal postulates
of the woman's movement.   Economic improvements
would have little effect in changing the real relations of
the sexes.   Even if a woman were able to gain her
living independently of man, still she would not be
free unless quite other influences began to operate in
her favour.

The female sex will never, the old idealist Hippel to
the contrary notwithstanding, be set on an equal footing

with the male merely as a result of "the magnanimity and sense of justice of man." Although, personally, I am absolutely convinced that these are the distinctive qualities of noble manhood, I still think that the world at large is moved by more elementary influences, and not by magnanimity or a sense of justice. That is true both of the ethical-psychological relations of the sexes and also of their relations in the economic affairs of life.

I mention this emphatically and at once in order to avoid the accusation that I have taken up the cudgels on behalf of the female sex against the male. Indeed, I have purposely avoided the question as to the superiority of one sex over the other. An unprejudiced judgment could be given only by a person who belonged to neither sex. Speaking for myself alone, and as a mere matter of subjective taste, I would give the preference to the male sex, but that seems to be a prejudice naturally inherent in the female.

To the majority of women as well as men, Kant's dictum on mankind in general will, unfortunately, apply all too well: "If you ask whether mankind is to be regarded as a good species or as a bad, I must confess that it has not much to boast about." Certainly, the ordinary woman has as little reason to boast as the ordinary man, and we ought to cease attempting to formulate any sweeping judgments about either sex as a whole. This method of generalisation is one of the vulgar mental habits of the present day which tend to confound the superior individual, the man who rises above the average, with the mass. The average man or woman, whether of the upper or of the middle class, is in no sense interesting, and the ordinary sex-characteristics do not make the study of either any more attractive. People begin to be interesting only when they differ from the ordinary type of their sex, when they are possessed of a certain individuality and emerge from the common rut. Then the vicissitudes of their lives attain a personal dignity, they are no longer commonplace, they have passed beyond the limitations of the type.

This book may be open to the accusation of dealing too much with exceptional examples, masculine and feminine, and it may also be said that, although such exceptions do occur, yet, broadly speaking, the differences between the sexes do not, as a rule, entitle us to question their validity.

What do we know of the psycho-sexual qualities of human beings, even of those with whom we are well acquainted? How difficult it is to lay bare the soul of man, so loth to allow itself to be examined, so swift to hide itself behind conventionalities as soon as it is conscious of being observed! And how crude and barbarous seem all our methods of expression when we approach that delicate, ethereal, manifold thing!

Is it possible for a man to be really understood when he differs from the ordinary run? Even when desirous to do so, would he be able to interpret himself to those from whom he differs? In ordinary intercourse with other men only the superficial and conventional aspects become visible, the inner and more personal traits are not revealed except to those of a similar temperament. That is the reason why the untypical remains so frequently unobserved, while the average type is supposed to be more common than it really is.

What should we have known of human nature if it had not been for the revelations of those who have shown themselves to us in their works? Such revela-

tions furnish the material which I have used with respect
to its symptomatic significance in the second part of the
book. It is the recognition of ideas, not their propagation, for which I have striven. I do not expect to convince opponents, for that would mean the conversion of
people of a different type, and I do not believe that
people of radically different temperaments can come to
any understanding by intellectual means. Even when
they are intellectually equal, they cannot approach one
another by reasonable argumentations, for all convictions—at least, all genuine convictions—are only the
outward expression of the inward nature. As a matter
of fact, men do not talk or write in order to carry conviction to other men, but only to express their own.
Those who are experienced in the subtleties of thinking
know that every sort of opinion may be asserted and
proved, and also doubted and controverted. The battle
of opinions, however thoroughly and by whatsoever
methods it may be carried on, is a mere idle game when
it does not indicate the expression of tendencies which
are vital to the individuality of the thinker.

I desire only that this book may come into the hands
of those who are akin to me through having similar
perceptions, and I hope that it will give them the kind
of pleasure that we all experience when we see reflected,
as in a mirror, the expression of our own inward feelings.

ROSA MAYREDER.

CONTENTS

OUTLINES

THE problem of sex psychology, and in particular of feminine psychology, centres in the question—Is woman condemned by her sex to a definitely circumscribed mentality or is there the same possibility of unlimited individual modifications in the feminine nature as in the masculine?

We get little light from theoretical researches as to how far mental sex differences affect the nature of various individuals. We merely learn that as great a variability exists among women as among men, and hence that within their physiological limits there is plenty of scope for the play of individuality. Decisive results cannot be expected, because those researches are carried out in a domain where the fundamental conceptions are still indefinite and dubious.

Psychology has come off very badly in the struggle between the spiritualistic and materialistic views, between the dualistic and monistic conceptions of the world, so characteristic of the intellectual life of the present day. When we have no certainty as to what is meant by Soul, Spirit, Reason, Intelligence or even Consciousness, when the most divergent views are taken of the relation between the soul and the body, how can any trustworthy data be obtained with regard to the sexual differentiation of the human " psyche " ?

no universal
male / female

The greatest confusion has been caused by the generalising methods which it has been customary to adopt. Such terms as " the male " and " the female " are employed as if they expressed some actual metaphysical entity existing in and distinguishing every man from every woman.

Yet it is evident that such generalisations have been drawn from experiences concerning merely a more or less extensive group of individuals, from experiences in which chance, prejudice or the subjective nature of the observer play too large a part. The contradictory ideas concerning " woman " that have in this way been launched into the world—for various reasons " man " has to a great extent been spared such ticketing—are so drastic in their effects because they pretend to have an objective value by virtue of these wide generalisations. From the literature on the theme of " woman " one obtains the odd impression that the character of one-half of mankind is strangely unknown, impenetrable, and enigmatic. Human beings who take part everywhere in the actualities of life, and whose natural qualities are similar to those of the male, are treated as fabulous animals, as proper subjects for myths and legends.

Conceptions of femininity are so wavering and indefinite that there is no common agreement as to what fundamental qualities are denoted by that word. This may best be shown by a collection of quotations from various authors, each of which may be taken as representative of views of which countless examples could be given. First, there is that view which considers pliancy and submission as the characteristic female qualities. Lombroso says this is due to a sense of

Stereotypes about women: (contradictions)

devotion, a sense which is always evolved in the relations between a lower and a higher being. George Egerton, on the other hand, considers that "an ancient insatiable desire for power is the motive force among women" and that in their eyes a man is only "a big, comical child."

Gentleness is so commonly considered as a feminine attribute that Virchow describes it as an "adjunct of the ovary." Havelock Ellis, however, affirms that nervous irritability is a characteristic which has always, and with justification, been assigned to the female. Another not less common conception is that woman likes stability and dislikes innovations. Möbius declares that "women are strongly conservative and hate all innovation" and Lombroso that "the history of legislation shows the peculiarly conservative tendency of women and its influence on social arrangements." And yet Hippel asserts that "the spirit of revolution broods over the female sex," and in Heine we find that "the element of freedom is always alive and active in the minds of women."

Bachhofer declares that "Law is innate in women, that to abide by it is their natural instinct," and William Hartpole Lecky is of the opinion that women are superior both in instinctive virtues and in those which arise from conviction and a sense of duty. Eduard von Hartmann, on the contrary, declares that the female sex is unjust and unfair. Schopenhauer considers that "unjustness is a fundamental trait of female character," and Lombroso has discovered "a half-criminaloid being even in the normal woman."

A very common view is expressed by Julius Düboc, "In all ages it has been an understood thing that women must not transgress the code of propriety—but propriety, of course, consists merely in keeping within the bounds recognised by the majority." The two brothers Goncourt declare, on the other hand, that "the chief strength of women consists in their power of going to extremes."

Kingsley apostrophises woman as "the only true missionary of civilisation, of fraternity, of tender, self-sacrificing love," but in the words of his fellow-countryman Pope, "every woman is at heart a rake."

Havelock Ellis considers that under ordinary circumstances a woman can do as much work as a man, but that she cannot work under high pressure; von Horn, in opposition to this, avers that "when it is a question of fulfilling very heavy requirements the female is often far superior to the male and shows a tenacity and endurance which put him to shame."

Lotze says that "the female hates analysis and is therefore incapable of distinguishing falsehood from truth"; but according to Lafitte: "the female prefers analysis, but the male the observation of the relations between things"; while according to Lombroso: "In synthesis and abstract reasoning the female intelligence is defective; its strength lies in acute analysis and in the vivid comprehension of details." Nietzsche, in contradiction to an almost unanimous opinion, says that those "who know how to discriminate . . . will perceive that women have intelligence and men emotion and passion."

The most opposed opinions prevail even with regard to the attitude of woman towards love, a subject which is certainly most intimately interwoven with her sexual peculiarities. Some authors insist that faithfulness is a fundamental principle in women, since the duties of motherhood cause them instinctively to seek permanence in love. To quote Krafft-Ebing: "Certainly the inward tendency of a woman's heart is towards monogamy, whilst man is inclined towards polygamy"; and Schopenhauer: "A man's love diminishes from the moment of its gratification; he longs for change. A woman's love, on the contrary, increases from that very moment. . . . He is constantly on the look-out for other women, but she clings steadfastly to the one man."

In opposition to this Lombroso may be quoted: "It is quite certain that when another relationship offers her greater practical advantages she will in the cruellest way leave her first love, and often without the least remorse"; and Laura Marholm records the opinion that "Woman likes change and variety; man thrives in that monotony which drives a woman to desperation." All these opinions are merely paraphrases of the phrase, "*La donna è mobile*"—the best-known formula for all the innumerable complaints about the fickleness and inconstancy of woman.

Contrary to the accepted opinion that female love consists in complete self-sacrifice ("a man's love is characterised by self-interest, a woman's by self-surrender"), M. de Lambert declares that "women play with love,—they give themselves up to it, but they do not give way to it." Friedrich Nietzsche has thus formulated the difference between the sexes in their attitude towards love: "A woman grows pale at the idea that the object of her affection might not be worthy of her, a man grows pale at the idea that he may not be worthy of the woman he loves." Goethe wrote to Frau von Stein: "I would I might be tried in triple

fire so that I might prove worthy of your love."
Mantegazza, however, drawing up a list of psychological
sex peculiarities makes the man ask exactly the opposite
question : " Is she worthy of me, can she satisfy me? "
while the woman asks: " Am I worthy of him, can I
satisfy him? "

It would not be difficult to multiply these examples
ad infinitum. We may add to them those that deny
any psychical difference between the sexes, for instance,
Broca: " Men and women, if left entirely to their own
inward tendencies, would grow to resemble one another
very closely, as indeed they do when in the savage
state." It was Montaigne's opinion that men and
women were very like one another in character; that
"apart from institutions and customs," he says, "the
difference between them was not great." Then we have
Grillparzer's phrase, " The noble woman is half, in fact,
wholly masculine "; and Brissac's " Souls have no sex ";
and Swift's " I do not know any amiable quality of
women which would not be equally amiable in a man.
I will not even except modesty and gentleness; neither
do I know any vice or folly which would not be equally
abhorrent in either sex." Lombroso, on the contrary,
considers every approximation of the female to the male
type—in spite of his previously expressed opinion that
pleasant women are often of a masculine type!—as a
sign of atavism; " before everything else we seek in
women for specifically feminine qualities, when we find
the opposite we consider it as a great anomaly."

What, then, are we to think of a subject upon which
every one has a different opinion, which is considered
by some as unimportant and subsidiary, by others as
one of the weightiest of normal criteria? After so

many paradoxical expressions and contrary opinions, should we not be finally justified in believing that one and all are merely the result of subjective tastes and conventional prejudices?

One good result of the woman's movement is that it has given an impulse to a critical examination of the whole question. As late as the first half of the nineteenth century a brilliant and subtle thinker like Ludwig Feuerbach dismissed the problem with the inane definition: "The essential quality of a man is manliness, of a woman, womanliness. . . . In what lie the virtue and efficiency of male humanity? In Manliness. Of female humanity? In Womanliness. The efficiency and health of humanity consist solely in this, that the female part should be as a woman ought to be and the male as a man ought to be."

In the present day the most superficial thinker would scorn to remain content with such utterances. Still, we cannot assume that the prevailing battle of opinions has as yet brought about a greater clearness and definiteness. The woman's movement, in order to be consistent, must regard these definitions of womanliness from a sceptical or even from a negative standpoint. It doubts or denies the value of these definitions, and in their place sets up unlimited freedom for individual development. It lays its entire stress on the spheres that are common to women and men and demands an independent consideration of each case regardless of normal sex peculiarities.

Perhaps this is the only rightful standpoint to hold with respect to the separate individual who comes into the world as a being with characteristics that cannot be altered. It is probably the only standpoint that can be maintained without depending on arbitrary suppositions. And if Heine is right in assuming that a desire for freedom is characteristic of the female sex, then the woman's movement may be regarded as genuinely female.

The problem of sex psychology will not, however, be solved by these means. It may merely be avoided. Those who make themselves independent of the normal conditions of womanhood do not thereby annul them. Although the limitations may be altered and the ideals may be changed, they still remain an important part of the mental life of mankind, they are the product of long evolution and of a culture that must not be undervalued.

This does not, however, imply that one must acknowledge its conventional value. There is always a danger in recognising conventional valuations, as has been lately revealed in the tendency to acknowledge a fundamental difference between the sexes, and to establish maternity as the determinative factor which is to limit woman's position in the sphere of future civilisation. Maternity may weigh as a heavy incumbrance upon women in the matter of their outward equality with man, but as regards their mental equality this generalisation is as little of a universal criterion as any other.

If we endeavour to obtain a concrete conception of what is meant by femininity we find three methods possible. We may assume the average woman to be the norm, or we may construct an ideal by taking physical qualities as parallels and analogues of the psychical, classing activity and passivity, productivity and receptivity as opposite types; or we may draw conclusions respecting psychical qualities from physiological attributes with which they must necessarily be connected.

By each of these methods a fictitious type is created and each of the sexes divided into two groups—a very large one consisting of the so-called normal and a very small one of the so-called abnormal individuals. But from the above quoted passages it may be seen that as regards womanliness the results of these three methods do not agree. Examples which, judged according to one method, would be characterised as abnormal would, under the others, be classified as normal, and *vice versâ*.

The method of averages seems to be quite inadequate. Apart from Philistine narrowness and subjective prejudices, sex-psychology does not concern itself with merely pointing out the well-known and ordinary signs from which general principles may be deduced. It attempts to discover some natural principle which is common to all females—that is to say to all complete females—in all periods and in all races. Such a principle would be most clearly recognisable in the females of animals other than human, because in them the despotism of human consciousness has not yet disturbed the incommunicable quality resident in natural manifestations.

Still less effective is the second method—that of judging the individual according to an ideal standard. Here we are confronted with two separate questions: firstly, what ought a woman to be? secondly, what, by virtue of her own nature, a woman actually is. At best, the idealisation could but furnish a criterion by which the worth of an individual woman could be estimated from an ethical and social standpoint; the question as to how far the differentiation between oppo-

site extremes might be desirable would remain un-
answered.   We must turn to the third method if we
wish to undertake an enquiry which shall be free from
arbitrary assumptions and prejudices.

II

ACCORDING to the fundamental hypotheses of modern
natural science, every indication of consciousness is
connected with some bodily manifestation.   It would
seem then that an actual psychic difference between the
sexes must be unconditionally affirmed.   If the physical
difference is so thorough that it is discernible even in
the hair, and "a man is a man even to his thumbs, and
a woman is a woman down to her little toes" (Ellis),
is it not clear in advance that the female body must
carry a soul quite different from that of the male body?
Ancient physiology has recorded the observation:
Totus homo semen est; modern physiology bears
this out.   "Woman is woman only through her genital
glands: all the peculiarities of her body and mind, of
her nutrition and nervous activity, the tender delicacy
and roundness of the limbs, with the peculiar enlarge-
ment of the pelvis, the development of the breasts when
the voice has attained its fulness, the beautiful head of
hair, together with the scarce perceptible down on the
rest of the skin, and then, in addition to all this, the
depth of feeling, truth of intuition, gentleness, devotion
and faithfulness—in short, everything which we admire
and honour in woman as truly womanly, is merely a
dependence of the ovary." (Virchow, *Das Weib und
die Zelle.*)
In this utterance of the great pathologist one is

struck by the sudden jump from the enumeration of so-called secondary sexual character to psychic qualities, the connection of which with sexual differences is so little evinced that other observers cite quite contrary attributes as typically feminine. Indeed, the " true woman " of Virchow, even in respect of secondary character—under which we understand recognisable physical peculiarities which accompany the sex, such as the cock's comb, the stag's antlers, the man's beard—does not agree with ethnographic facts or even with the varying taste of civilised nations. Thus the men of civilised races have a wider, therefore a more feminine, pelvis than the women of more savage stock, while the men of such stock share the " beautiful head of hair " with civilised women; the tendency to grow hair on the upper lip is recognised as a race-mark of Portuguese, Spanish and Hungarian women; and as for the rounding of the limbs and the development of the breasts, the newest fashionable ideal of the female figure, which has been called the " animated skeleton," differs considerably from the Virchow ideal. Whether this fashion be a perversion or no, does not come into consideration, but solely the fact that the constitution of many women corresponds with this ideal. The mere variability of taste, through which a definite variation is exalted to a ruling type, should warn us to hesitate in accepting any conception of the " true woman."

In more recent times there have been extensive investigations on the subject of the physiological peculiarities whieh in general constitutionally distinguish woman from man. As the best known works of this sort might be mentioned *Woman as a Criminal and Prostitute*, by Lombroso and Ferrero, and *Man and*

Woman, by Havelock Ellis.   The Englishman's book, which is preferable to the much-contested work of the Italian authors, because of its systematic arrangement and critical method, contains a conscientious and penetrating comparison of all the exact scientific results in this direction.   Everything in the human organism that can be measured and weighed is here carefully considered in relation to its psycho-sexual importance.   Yet the author is obliged to confess at the end of his work: "We have not succeeded in determining the radical and essential characters of men and women uninfluenced by external modifying conditions. . . . By showing us that under varying conditions men and women are, within certain limits, indefinitely modifiable, a precise knowledge of the actual facts of the life of men and women forbids us to dogmatise rigidly concerning their respective spheres.   It is a matter which experience alone can demonstrate in detail. . . . And so many of the facts are modifiable under a changing environment that in the absence of experience we cannot pronounce definitely regarding the behaviour of either the male or female organism under different conditions."

As these investigations are only concerned with establishing facts such as are to be obtained by means of scientific methods of observation and statistical calculations, it is clear that in this way one stops short at the symptoms without being able to penetrate to their source.   Biogenetical research dives deeper into the nature of sexual differentiation.

The physiological functions of nutrition and propagation evidence even in the most primitive organisms two tendencies of vital activity, one inwardly accumulative, and the other outwardly distributive.   These original tendencies express the peculiarities of the male and female germ cells; and the preponderance of one of these tendencies determines in the embryo a prodigal or a thrifty constitution, a masculine or a feminine polarisation. The masculine polarisation gives, as the properties of the germ-cell show, mobility, energy, initiative, the inclination to sweep afar and the ability to assert oneself under unfavourable conditions. The feminine postulates stability, passive self-dependence, an inclination to be firm and shut off from outside influences (see Feuillet, *The Psychology of the Sexes and its Biological Foundation*). If we pursue these deductions further, then we may say that the choleric-sanguine temperament presents itself as the masculine, the phlegmatic-lymphatic as the feminine temperament; the male sex embodies the progressive or centrifugal element that renews and transforms the species, the female sex the conservative or centripetal, that maintains and preserves the species unchanged.

Here we seem to have a firm foundation for what may be considered as psychic sex-characteristics, and taken for granted in all sexually differentiated individuals. But in reality we have only created a type from which every individual differs more or less. The most superficial observation will show that these general definitions are not even true of persons who in no particular are extraordinary, that in many cases the individual differences contradict the general difference. Thus it is not difficult to find individuals whose psychic-sexual characteristics are reversed, although physically they may be normal representatives of their sex. But here lies the real problem: If the germ-cell presents the only and exclusive principle of the constitution of the organism, how are such deviations possible? and if the physical sex-difference does not necessarily determine the spiritual character of the individual, what factors are the cause of these deviations?

But apart from untypical individuals, these generalisations from biological facts leave unexplained a whole row of phenomena that concerns natural lines of development. There are many breeds of animals, among them some of the higher kinds, whose somatic character, outside the actual sphere of sex, seems to be quite independent of the nature of the germ-cells. Mare and stallion, dog and bitch, for example, among which one can scarcely find secondary sexual characteristics, do not differ intellectually according to their sex. Thus race-horses and hunting hounds are used without regard to sex. With these the mobility, energy, and initiative which are supposed to belong exclusively to the masculine germ-cell, are distributed equally between both sexes. Indeed, the bees show us that a reversal of the sex characteristics may become the rule. In the community of the bee the social life of the sexes is in direct contradiction to the character which the germ-cell is supposed to have given them. The male drone distinguishes himself by his fondness for a lazy, retired existence from the active, busy, and adventurous female worker bee.

The explanation of this may, of course, be found in the nature of the germ-cells themselves. According to recent investigations into the self-contained capacity of these for sex differentiation, it is highly probable that the female germ-cell has in its own constitution a masculine polarisation, that is to say, it decides the

"germ-cell" & characteristics.

generation of a male organism; the male germ-cell on the contrary, a feminine polarisation, that is to say, it decides the generation of a female organism. Observation of the very peculiar conditions of propagation obtaining among the bees shows that the unfertilised eggs exclusively produce drones, that is, males; but that the female bees—who may become workers or queens according to the nature of their food—can only be produced with the co-operation of the masculine generative matter (see Janke, *Die willkürliche Hervorbring- ung des Geschlechtes*) (*The Voluntary Determination of Sex*).

If, then, the female organism begets masculine germs, the male organism feminine germs, why should not this capacity also express itself in the character of the soul of which it is the vehicle? Moreover, Lourbet (*The Problem of the Sexes*) has pointed out that the characteristic signs of the female " psyche " could have been deduced from the qualities of the masculine germ-cell : " for woman is livelier and quicker of thought than man, unstable, nervous and incapable of anything which requires perseverance and endurance." Thus the tendency of the masculine germ-cell to a complete abnegation of its own being and fusion with a larger, self-contained organism like the ovulum, may be pointed to as a sign of that inclination to surrender and self- sacrifice which has always been considered a particular distinguishing feature of the female nature.

No sure foundation for a psychological formula of Femininity is to be found here. On a closer examina- tion we find little more than arbitrary suppositions in which everything points in a direction agreeable to the writer, especially with reference to the type which experience has rendered familiar, or to which the prevalent views incline him.

While we are trying to explain masculinity and femininity in their contemporary aspects by means of original and primitive organic conditions, we are liable to overlook the fact that in many essential respects they are products of civilisation, and in no sense permanent, conclusive, or generally significant. Among most savage peoples the division of labour between man and woman is quite different from that among civilised nations. Nearly everywhere it is the women who are the first burden-bearers, the first tillers of the soil, the first builders and the first potters—if, indeed, the whole industrial part of primitive life, together with the first inventions belonging thereto, may not be said to be the work of the female sex (see Ellis, *Man and Woman*). Presumably the physiological observation of these primitive women would yield results in many respects differing from those of civilised women.

But if we limit ourselves to psycho-sexual phenomena within the limits of European civilisation, we must bear in mind one fact of the utmost importance in many ways, namely, the relatively greater degree of individual differentiation.

It is a distinguishing peculiarity of man that his sexual bent varies according to the individual and is not uniform, as among the animals. The degree of masculinity or femininity of a lion, a horse or a hare is determined by its breed. Taken by herself, a lioness is a more masculine animal than a roebuck, inasmuch as it is generally accepted that aggressive impulse is a sign of masculinity. But among the highest mammals one begins to notice signs of individual differentiation; and among human races it is only among the most primitive that the sexes are divided into comparatively homogeneous groups.

With the increase of civilisation, under favourable conditions and in freer social circumstances, the human unit begins to expand individually—perhaps because under conditions of assured safety the sway of society lessens, and the pressure which it exerts upon its members no longer indicates the necessity of self-preservation, and therefore is no longer regarded as inviolable. This may be so because the adaptation to the conditions of sexual selection, which made primitive woman the involuntary object of robbery or purchase, has itself altered with the conditions. The fulness and freedom of the development of outward things proceeds parallel with the fulness and development of inward things. Nature herself, an eternal progression from simple and primitive forms to forms ever more complicated and more perfect, from the uniform to the multiform, evidences itself in the human race as a progression from the typical to the individual.

Qualities which, looked at individually and alone, might appertain as much to one sex as to the other, create in their combinations the individualised personality. The extraordinary diversity of these combinations in itself constitutes an objection to considering personality merely as a reflection of sex, and to regarding man and woman in their spiritual characters merely as paraphrases of their sexual machinery. Is it really possible by means of such simple things as the formation of the germ-cells or the processes of nutrition and assimilation to explain the conscious powers of an organism so complicated as that of man?

III

ALL methods yield only percentages, and divide the sexes into majorities and minorities. Thus, almost without exception, all weight is given to the character of the majorities. And yet minorities are by no means unimportant or superfluous in the social scheme, and they are responsible for many changes and developments of civilised society.

But let us leave that matter on one side for the 'moment. Let us first investigate the fact that the psychic character of single individuals—irrespective of the fact whether these be rare or frequent—does not correspond with their sexual type.

Lombroso has put forward <u>the law of crossed transmission in explanation of untypical femininity.</u> "Such women are perhaps the product of a peculiar mechanism of heredity; they seem to have derived their sexual organs and secondary sexual characteristics from the mother and their brains from the father; paradoxical mixtures of this sort likewise postulate the type of the effeminate man." He is also of the opinion that, inasmuch as the female sex is the less variable, only the domain of normality or extreme anomaly seems represented by it, and that the innumerable transitional forms which unite these two poles are wanting. This is one of many arbitrary and unproved assertions which show how purely subjective is the standpoint of Lombroso. The crossed transmission from which such "paradoxical mixtures" derive, belongs to the fundamental laws which, according to the Darwinian Theory, determine the character of the species. We know that the law of

the direct transmission of secondary sexual characteristics and sexual organs from the male organism to the
male offspring and from the female organism to the
female offspring, is limited and partly suspended by the
law of mixed or amphigonous hereditary transmission.
"This law declares that every individual organism
generated by sexual means derives peculiarities from
both parents." (Haeckel, *Natural History of Creation*.)

It is frequently observed that daughters more frequently resemble their father, sons more frequently their
mother. In all probability a father might sooner expect
to find his own peculiarities in his daughters than in
his sons. On this fact—which contains an illustration
of the capacity of the germ-cell to produce its sexual
opposite—Janke has founded a scheme of heredity by
which the true heir and copy of the father is the daughter's son, while a woman lives on in her son's daughters.
The true male descent of a family thus does not, as at
present accepted, proceed from father to son, but in a
cross line from father to daughter and daughter to
grandson.

Schopenhauer, too, in his analysis of existence, has
deduced a theory according to which will is the primary
and intellect the secondary principle, and postulates a
sort of crossed transmission in which he makes the male
sex, as primary, the hereditary bearer of character, the
female, as the secondary, the bearer of hereditary intellectual endowment. In his *Republic* he emphasises the
fact that in order to ensure the raising of a posterity as
sound as possible, the men of strongest character must
be united to the most intelligent women. Incidentally,
this theory of Schopenhauer's is an example of how little
a preconceived opinion is to be shaken by the results of

observation; for the instances in which character and intellect are not transmitted at all in the given manner are so numerous and conspicuous that Schopenhauer himself would have been unable to overlook them—if he had not had his little theory!

The fact of <u>crossed transmission</u> already makes it evident that the single individual unites in himself masculine and feminine qualities, and cannot, even in the lowest degree of development, be considered as a "homologous sexual being." One might, indeed, found on this a conception that each individual presents a mixture, that absolute masculinity and femininity never occur. By the adoption of a principal of sex gradation individual deviations from the general type could then be explained.

But the theory of sex gradation, however alluring in itself, does not offer a good starting point for that which really lies beyond the primary sphere of sex, or derivative interpretations—that is to say, the real meaning of what is masculine and what feminine. As such a starting point is not to be arrived at by physiological-biological methods, we must either begin with the results of averages, which are a sum of superficial observations, or commit what the philosophers call a *petitio principii* and start with an ideal. For it is only arbitrary supposition to call all positive qualities masculine and all negative qualities feminine, since experience shews them to be common in both sexes.

It was Schopenhauer who pointed out the different degrees in the sexual character of individuals, and made use of this gradual differentiation of sex in explanation of the phenomena of love. In his *Metaphysics of Love*, he says, "All sex is one-sidedness. This one-sidedness is expressed more decidedly in one individual than in another, and may therefore be complemented and neutralised by one individual rather than by another. . . . The physiologists know that manhood and womanhood allow of countless differences of degree, by means of which the one sinks to the level of some repugnant Gynander and Hypospadiaens, and the other is elevated into some charming Androgyne. Both sides may reach a perfect Hermaphroditism, where stand those individuals who, halting midway between the sexes, belong to neither, and are therefore useless for propagation."

Schopenhauer was content with describing sex gradation as a physiological phenomenon; he did not take into consideration the fact that physiological sexual constitution can be no criterion of psychic character, because individuals who physically represent very pronounced sexual types are often psychically quite untypical and fail to correspond at all with their physique.

Otto Weininger, in his book, *Sex and Character*, has sought much deeper in his efforts to grasp the problem of sex gradation. He starts with the assumption that every cell of the organism possesses a sex character or a decided sexual accentuation. It is true he is obliged to confess "in what the masculinity (Maskulität) or the femininity (Muliebrität) of a cell may actually consist, . . . it is impossible at present to state definitely or with any degree of probability." He traces the sexual character of each cell to a modification of that hypothetical Idioplasma which gives to every tissue the specific character of the species. He divides this Idioplasma into "Arrhenoplasma," bearer of the masculine, and "Thelyplasma," bearer of the feminine principal. In every actual individual these two plasms are united

critique of weininger

in greater or lesser proportions: "An individual A or B should therefore no longer be described as simply 'Man' or 'Woman,' but each according to the fractions which they may possess of each other. This limits the supposed exclusive importance of the external sexual parts, "by which alone the sex of man and, to some degree, his destiny (not seldom unjustifiably, as will be shown), is in consequence decided."

In order to complete the original sex traits already qualified by the proportions of Arrheno and Thelyplasma, Weininger assumes—as others have done before him—an inner secretion of the germinal-glands, by means of which the sex of the individual is finally completed, so that sexual differentiation might also be explained as a chemical phenomenon.

The significance of Weininger's hypothesis lies principally in the endeavour to create a biological Formula for the infinite many-sidedness of individual development, and thus avoid the false inferences which arise from the dependence upon general types. The designations Arrheno and Thelyplasma do not, to be sure, decide the essence of masculine and feminine; for as both appear in either sex, only in varying proportions, one is unable to perceive in this the constituent principle of sex differentiation. Weininger assumes a hypothetical division of the protoplasm, and thus helps himself over the difficulty in the same way as the physiologists who explain the phenomenon of consciousness by ascribing it to the protoplasm. In both cases the problem is not solved; it is merely pushed one step farther in advance.

As soon as Weininger gives up the biologico-psychological method of consideration which he pursues in the first part of his work, and takes up the psychologio-philosophical, he finds himself compelled, since no criterion can be obtained from his hypothesis, to make use of the general type in order to give the first application of his gradation theory. Indeed, in the second part he completely annuls the suppositions of the first, in order to introduce, by means of the method of logical deduction, unexceptionally valid criteria for man and woman. But the recognition of sex gradation—by which Weininger understands, not a graduated approach to physical hermaphroditism, but degrees of constitution outside the primary sphere of sex—excludes these unexceptionable valid criteria, because they are rooted in the conception that the primary division of the sexes does not extend to the complex total of the qualities that are united in an individual personality. In the construction of his general type—which he calls a " platonic idea "—Weininger uses as a standard of femininity the " most trivial experience " and " the commonest and most superficial things," while for masculinity he simply gathers together all the highest mental and moral attributes, thus dividing the sexes into extreme antitheses, he comes naturally to very different conclusions than those that would have resulted from building on his theory of gradation. He goes so far as to assert that " even the lowest man stands infinitely higher than the highest woman," because only man is a monad, only he has a soul; woman, on the contrary, is soulless, possesses no ego and no individuality, has neither personality nor freedom, neither character nor will. Indeed, he even declares that " women "—observe, " women," and not a mere abstraction of woman—" have no existence and no essence, they are not—they are nothing."

According to the postulates of the original biologico-psychological observation, it would at least have been difficult to avoid the question: At what degree of masculinity does the soul begin? For if man alone possesses a soul then the masculine Idioplasm or Arrhenoplasm must be reckoned as the physical correlative of the soul, and must to a certain degree be found mixed with the constitution of the feminine individual. When Weininger denies a soul to even the most masculine woman, that is to say, the woman with a large proportion of Arrhenoplasm, but grants it to the most feminine man, he fetters the soul to the most primary sexual feature, and involuntarily exalts the phallus as the vehicle of the soul. By the roundabout way of an apparently very pithy biological theory, and with expenditure of an enormous amount of mental labour, Weininger's doctrine of gradation arrives at the ancient, clumsy, psychologically undifferentiated view which segregates men and women according to their primary sexual features into two widely separated antitheses.

In this insufficiency of principle and failure of the basic problem, Weininger's work shows that the problem of sexual psychology remains insoluble so long as the sexual antithesis is regarded as an essential separation and a radical difference, permeating the whole constitution as well as the psychic personality.

IV

WHAT real biological necessity is there for the separation of the sexes? In the lowest grades of life they are one. The protoplasm, the first manifestation of organic life, shows no sign of an elementary separation, and the earliest forms of animal life are sexually undivided. If the impulse towards separation lay in matter itself, there could be no sexless living object.

The separation of the sexes is achieved through certain conditions of development in a chain of the most varied and fluctuating forms. In his *Love-life in Nature*, William Bölsche gives a clear picture of this process of development, the determining causes of which are to be found in that hereditary transmission which plays the most important part in propagation. In so far as the separation of the sexes serves the interests of propagation, so far does it determine the organisation of the individual. But the individual, especially of the higher species, has a life of its own that remains untouched by the purposes of propagation. Science is unable to point out a sexual differentiation in the greater number of the organs that serve this life. So far-reaching a differentiation, considerably overstepping her purpose, is contrary to Nature's economy. So that the differences which sex brings with it must be held to be only relative and unable to influence the constitution sufficiently to alter the character of the race. For if there are primitive organisms in which the sexes differ so widely that male and female appear as if belonging to different species, this may be considered as one of the numberless possibilities to which sex differentiation is subject in adopting itself to external circumstances— one of those possibilities which in other cases are responsible for the complete sexual similarity of individuals uniting in propagation, as, for example, snails.

Concerning the natural purpose of sex-differentiation and its biological significance, Weismann declares : " Of an equally secondary nature with the differentiation of cells into masculine and feminine reproductory cells, is that of personal units into male and female; and all the numberless differences in form and function which characterise sex among the higher animals . . . are nothing but adaptations in order to produce the mingling of the hereditary tendencies of two individuals."

Individuals, then, will differ according to their sex most strongly in those peculiarities which are immediately connected with the problem of propagation. These peculiarities may be described as a *teleological differentiation of sex.* If we take into account the psychological disposition which accompanies human sexuality as a parallel phenomenon, this teleological differentiation in man would thus be found in all those qualities which favour sexual conquest—in the aggressive temperament which predisposes him to a warlike, enterprising and violent existence, and in case of the woman, in the weak-willed, patient, unenterprising nature which favours passivity and makes her fitter for the conception, bearing, and rearing of offspring. We ought to mean nothing more than the teleological weakness of woman and the teleological strength of man when we speak of specifically feminine and specifically masculine qualities. *They comprise the suitability of the individual's psychic constitution for the achievement of his duty to the species.*

These qualities which serve solely to determine the sex of the individual belong to the domain of the primitive sex-nature. But by means of that which, ever since there has been a spiritual and moral development of man, has been understood as his " higher nature," or even through individual deviations from the teleological type, the psychic constitution encroaches more or less on this domain. The relation of the individual to the general differentiation and its independence of the primitive sex-nature, suggest that a thorough agreement of all organs in the direction of sexual polarity by no means exists.

Every higher animal organism is a compound and complex mechanism. The higher its place in the scale of development the more complicated its formal and functional organisation. The explanation of the fact that sex has not that decisive influence over the whole of the organism that is so frequently attributed to it, lies possibly in the physiological conditions of its origin. A sketch of its ontogenetic history—in approximate outlines—will make that clear.

With the increasing growth of the fertilised egg-cell three layers are formed, by which one perceives even at this stage that the future organs have their origin in separate groups of cells. Thus out of the outer layer (ectoderm) arise the nervous system and spinal cord, also the organs of sense and the epidermis, with their respective glands; out of the inner layer (entoderm) the principal organs of vegetative glandular activity, the lungs, liver, pancreas, kidneys, etc., in so far as the groups of cells that serve the special vegetative processes are concerned; the middle layer (mesoderm) provides all the apparatus for movement and support which the organs derived from the other layers require for their growth, also the organs for the circulation of the blood, and for movement—muscles, bones, cartilage, and sinews. The mesoderm is at the same time the layer out of which the sexual organs are formed (see Ranke's *Man*).

These layers represent three different and relatively independent groups of cells; and the human organism that is produced by their amalgamation remains to the tenth week of its embryonic existence a hermaphrodite creature, which does not acquire sex, that is the potential capacity to reproduce, until the most important organs for its own personal life have been formed. The fact that the most important of all, the brain and the spinal cord, possess that peculiar autonomy by virtue of which the whole central nervous system may, in a certain sense, be termed a self-dependent and separate organism within our organism (Ranke), might, perhaps, be ascribed to the circumstance that it arises from a different germ layer from the organs of generation and attains its first development at a time when the latter are not even in existence.

Concerning the causes which decide the sex of the embryo, in spite of numerous hypotheses—at the beginning of the last century there were about three hundred of them and modern science has considerably increased them—complete uncertainty prevails. The assumption that the sex is already decided in procreation is opposed by the assumption that it is determined in the course of embryonic development, and principally through the influence of nutrition. As both these hypotheses are confirmed by the experiments and observations of their supporters, without offering any reliability in the arbitrary determination of sex, it is not impossible that one or the other may sometimes be the case. Either one of the germ-cells itself decides the sex by its own internal tendency, or both in their fusion are neutralised, in which case the sex either remains indeterminate, as in hermaphrodites, or is determined afterwards by other influences encountered by the new organism during its development. In the latter case especially the organs that derive from the ectoderm and entoderm maintain their independence of the subsequent sex differentiation.

For a long time the decisive factor of spiritual sex difference was sought in the brain, and it was believed that many signs thereof had been found. But to-day there can no longer be any doubt that the human brain exhibits merely individual and not sexual differences. After many futile endeavours to recognise sex by the weight or shape of the brain, modern anatomy has given up the hope of contributing any documents to the problems of the psychology of sex by this means.

Only as a figure of speech may one speak of a "masculine brain"—say, in a woman whose intelligence is above the ordinary. Physiologically, this expression is as meaningless as Ulrich's well-known formula in explanation of the phenomenon of contrary sexual emotion: *Anima mulieris in corpore virili inclusa*—at bottom only a circumscription of the fact that the sexual feelings of the female may be united with an externally complete masculine organism. This remarkable abnormality, which is not yet clear in its causes, suggests that not only the brain in its entirety, but the cerebral centre which brings the sex impulse into consciousness, is independent in its development of the sexual glands. Krafft-Ebing, who, in other matters of sexual psychology, assumes entirely the conventional point of view, says in this connection: "It is an interesting question, . . . whether the psycho-sexual development is determined by the peripheral influences of the genital glands or by central cerebral conditions," and lays stress on the fact that the local precedents in the sexual organs "are only accessory and not exclusive factors in the growth of a psycho-sexual personality." It may serve as an illustration of this, that the castration of men by no means achieves the thorough change in sex characteristics that is commonly presupposed (see Möbius, *Castration*).

If the origin of the brain in a particular layer is not without importance for the individual differentiation, the *rôle* of the mesoderm, as the layer immediately concerned with the formation of sex, seems decisive for the sexual typification of the individual. Inasmuch as it supplies form, carriage, movement and connection with the rest of the body to those organs whose functional part is supplied by the other layers, it becomes the "principal factor in the building-up of the whole body." Out of this relationship of the generative layer to the organs, whose form it influences without having a part in their specific character, the difference in the bodily appearance of the sexes is explained. The general differences between the sexes, which are not only an essential but a secondary difference, are here most pointedly expressed.

In this physical analogy we may perhaps soonest obtain a starting point for what may in a figurative sense be called masculinity and femininity, without having to force the facts of individual differentiation by means of unjustified averages. As the bodily appearance of the sexes, both of which bear the common marks of the race, consists in a formal difference, so does also the psychological sex-difference, examined to its furthest extent, consist in a formal quality.

V

WE have seen that it is not possible to point to a natural principle in sex-differentiation, a principle which of necessity stipulates a definitely circumscribed constitution of being; likewise that physiological and biological methods always lead to the grouping of individuals into majorities and minorities, but are incapable of setting up an unexceptionable type. In addition, we have followed, in the sense of the unlimited freedom of individuality, those instances which permit of the conclusion that sexual differentiation imposes no limits on individual differentiation.

But on no account should it be said that the sexes are not in many cases, perhaps in most cases, to be distinguished by spiritual and intellectual peculiarities. It means nothing more than that these psychic sex characteristics are not necessarily bound up with the sex; that in a certain number of individuals, and those often excellent and distinguished representatives of their sex, they are either wanting or even transposed into the opposite traits. This only means that the sexual differentiation in the majority of individuals extends over a greater psychic domain. The more primitive an individual, the more the teleological qualities of the sex will preponderate in his spiritual economy, since propagation is a matter of greater importance in primitive life. In the higher degrees of individual differentiation and in proportion to the fulness of the inner life, the domination of sex-teleology takes a secondary place, inasmuch as, as a phenomenon of adaptation, it is itself changed and fitted to the altered conditions of life.

Indeed, there are also individuals spiritually very

distinguished, in whom the narrower sphere of sex remains undifferentiated. The fact that the so-called sexual virtues take the first place in the social valuation of the sexes should not mislead us into considering them so generally distributed and of such worth as those who look upon every untypical individual as an "anomaly" would wish. The examination of the background of these social valuations is a separate study; the fact that they are so frequently (without further criticism) made the basis of what is "normal" in matters of the psychology of sex is only a sign that philosophical thought is not always a protection against philistine narrowness.

The nature of the individuality must in every single instance be separated from the conventional picture that represents the sexual type to current human knowledge. Even in the sphere of erotics, where the generally accepted characteristics of man and woman as "active" and "passive" have strongest sway, a careful analysis will discover the individual differences to be as great as in the rest of the psychic domain. Anyone who is not misled by the formal peculiarities in the appearance of the sexes knows how much importance need be attached to the idea that the man is always the wooing party; and it does not need long observation to remark how little attraction is actually exercised by a completely passive femininity.

That which is generally understood as the normal conception of femininity, the teleological sex nature, can, from the point of view of a higher conception of life, give no clue for the individual. The value of this normative idea, looked at in its relation to the unit, is not in the matter of its content; not in the determination and completion of internal conditions. It is not as a moral foot-rule—as a wide-spread but gross mistake would have it—that this understanding becomes a valuable product of the work of civilisation. But regarded as a definite and decisive principle, then sexuality obtains a far-reaching, if not exceptionless, applicability without coming into collision with the claims of individual freedom, which suffer no limitation from standards of the average.

If after we have stripped off all the influences of mode of life and occupation, of custom and extraction and freedom, judgment from conventional prejudices, and particularly from our own subjective tendency, we seek justification for all that may still be called manly or unmanly, womanly or unwomanly, then we will find at the bottom of our consciousness a feeling difficult to define. Taking concrete examples as guides, it seems quite clear that this feeling is not directed against certain qualities. We do not regard as unfeminine the great women of history or literature—a Portia, Arria, or Charlotte Corday, though their actions exhibit all the energy, resolution and courage of a particularly masculine temperament; nor as " unmanly " the loving resignation, gentleness and self-sacrifice by which many of the saints of Christian legends evince a distinctly feminine disposition. From this alone it is evident that in the higher ranks of personal perfection the ordinary psycho-sexual categories are no longer applicable. These divisions are more concerned with the externals of personality and the lower ranks of ordinary life. They leave unregarded an entire list of qualities which point to a personal distinction beyond all sex, as, for example, strength of mind, force of will, steadfastness, courage, reliability, etc. And in the moral ideal which Christen-

dom has given to the world, chastity, humility, peace-
fulness, even the need of subordination to the guidance
of a higher will, are all set forth as virtues irrespective
of sex.

The fact that a feminine personality affects us differently from a masculine lies not so much in *what* she
is as in *how* she is, in the kind and manner of her being.
Thence it happens that a woman may make an impression of complete womanliness in her appearance, although
her personal qualities differ entirely from those of the
average type of her sex.   A woman with the bearing
of ordinary masculinity is, to be sure, repellent under
all circumstances, as is also a man of womanish habits
and ways.   In this sense is meant the saying of Goethe,
" one should not divest oneself too greatly of the
costumes of the world and the period in which one lives,
and a woman should not wish to divest herself of her
womanliness."   Here womanliness is spoken of as a
garment of the mind.   As a product of civilisation,
meant to have a normative value over all individual
differences, it is nothing more than an æsthetic principle.
If it merely extends to appearance and surface, this
principle is certainly of as great an importance here as
elsewhere.

A very significant proof of the extent to which the
idea of femininity is influenced by formal considerations may be found in racial differences.   For example,
among Latin women the specifically feminine qualities
are much more marked than among their northern
sisters.   This goes so far that the womankind of certain
districts of North Germany, where the prevailing type
is lean, sinewy and big-boned, and of a serious and
untractable nature, are often reproached by Frenchmen

and, indeed, by South Germans, with the saying that they are " not women at all "—although the men of their own race consider them worthy representatives of femininity. In fact, the difference between a Parisienne and one of these North German women is perhaps greater than between the latter and men of a small, trim build and a gentle, gay, amiable nature, such, for example, as are not infrequently found in the Austrian army.

That which distinguishes civilised man from the savage is not, in the last analysis, his form—to treat as a secondary matter the racial ideal which is held and propagated by tradition is to under-rate one of the most valuable products of civilisation. Particularly women of culture, who owe so much to æsthetic principle, and in whom it takes so high a place, have every reason to treasure the formal idea of femininity as the normal one. To emancipate oneself from the ethical normative of femininity, which fetters individuality because of the teleological limits of sex, is a distinct right. But to preserve its formal quality is the task of a free personality.

The contradictions alone, that make the domain of sexual psychology a labyrinth of unsolved differences of opinion, go to prove that masculinity and femininity as a manner and form of being are compatible with the most widely differing qualities. The conceptions that every individual has of the constitution of the other sex are based not merely on form, but undoubtedly on certain qualities of being. But that offers no objection. For these conceptions are of a purely subjective nature; they are for the most part derived from a personal bias that demands in the nature of the other sex opposite and complementary qualities. They cannot serve as objective measures of psycho-sexual peculiarities because they are so variable and contradictory, as is in the nature of everything individual.

This conception of femininity as a form of being, and not as a kind of being, will therefore only satisfy that group of people who in advance, true to their individual bent, regard the spiritual sexual difference as something immaterial; but it will not satisfy those who, through their individual disposition or, to put it more plainly, through their erotic tastes, are forced to seek in the other sex a *toto genere* different being.

In conclusion, now that we have opened an unlimited perspective to the freedom of individuality and have, despite this, assured a normative value to the conception of femininity, nothing hinders us from once more explicitly emphasising the fact that the majority of women are, neither in the qualities of character nor of intellect, the equal of man. Indeed, this fact is not to be denied; and it weighs heavily, very heavily on the lives of those women who do not belong to the majority of their sex.

MOTHERHOOD AND CULTURE

IT will always be a clumsy proceeding to apply the method of averages to an individual in order to trace out the lines of his development or to decide *a priori* the limitations of his nature. But having conceded that the majority-type of the female sex differs in nature from that of the male, one must set forth the consequences of this phenomenon. In doing so, generalisations drawn from the average are unavoidable; but be it premised that every generalisation is to be received with caution, because the scope of its application is only in breadth, not in depth. The more general an assertion is, the more general must be its application. For example: it may be said that woman is the child-bearing part of mankind; but when one proceeds to the formula, "the vocation of woman is to become a mother," one oversteps the bounds of the generalisation, in that a new idea—that of vocation—is introduced, from which individual constituents cannot be eliminated.

With this reservation, then, we concede that the female majority-type is not the equal of the male either in intellect or in strength of will.

As to the causes of this, opinions are strongly opposed. They are sought on the one hand in environment, in education, and in the consequences of a subjection which has lasted for thousands of years; on the other hand,

37

vs anti-feminists

in the predestined nature and calling of woman and the limitations appertaining to motherhood. These limitations are innate, according to this view; they are involved by the burden of motherhood; but according to the opposite theory man, not Nature, is responsible for making motherhood into a drag-chain interfering with the spiritual and intellectual development of the female sex. The influence of environment and education and of the age-long subjection of woman has resulted only in secondary sex-differences which are really attributable merely to the male inclination to dominate over the female.

It is, however, quite unnecessary to agree with either the one point of view or the other—despite the fact that both are recognised as being opposite and as forming, respectively, the arguments of the Feminists on one hand and of the anti-Feminists on the other—for it is unmistakably true that the prevailing female type has to a considerable extent been determined by both of these influences.

He who wishes to form a just estimate of woman and her place in the spiritual life and culture of the world, can by no means afford, when estimating her achievements, to neglect her predestination to maternity. The " equality " of the sexes in general is something which one should consider only in so far as it stands in relation to the right of individual self-development—the absolute measure of comparison should only be used in cases where it is necessary to give judgment between two competitors of different sexes in one single contingency. None but the most partisan spirit, prejudiced either for or against, would fail to acknowledge that any equal achievement of the woman ought to be valued, subjectively, in a far higher degree, because of the greater difficulties, from within and from without, which she must overcome. Indeed, it may be said that one of the greatest acts of injustice that may be charged against those who uphold a supposedly objective valuation lies in comparing the feminine intellectuality in a historical sense with the masculine—making use of man himself as a masculine standard.

Even in the nature of those sexual relations which serve as preliminaries to motherhood, there is for woman something essentially fettering—a disposition towards bondage and subordination. Nature has made ample provision against any evasion by the individual of his duties to the race. With man she has assumed the performance of these duties through an aggressive desire; with woman, in cases where sexual impulses do not happen to have an aggressive tendency, she has achieved the same result by means of a peculiar weakness of will and a susceptibility to suggestion which subject her to the influence of the masculine will. This susceptibility to suggestion is an intrinsic factor in sexual conquest, and of this Nature has made full use as a means of more easily delivering the woman into the power of the man than would be possible if the same strength of will existed on both sides. Speaking generally and according to the evidence of the majority of cases, it is not man who falls into the power of woman because of the strength of her sex-impulses, but rather the woman who is overpowered by him. Indeed, so antagonistic is even his psychical attitude towards the temporary dependence under which he is of necessity placed because of the mutual nature of the sexual act, that this dependence becomes endurable to him only through the operation of certain ideas of property and mastership. The same mutuality in the case of the woman is attended by a feeling of submission and dependence.

The interests of the female sex would in no wise be furthered were one to overlook these obvious facts, despite the individual cases in which an equality of birth and intellectual equipment manifests itself as an example of the possibilities of evolution. Just as the teleological power which is granted to man as a sexual being is of advantage to him as a civilised being, so, in a like degree, as human existence grows farther and farther from its original and primitive state, does woman suffer in proportion to her teleological weakness.

It is true that certain lofty phenomena of the soul-life of humanity have their origin in teleological characteristics. The maternal instincts of the female and the warlike instincts of the male sex furnish a soil in which, under certain circumstances, thrive the most wonderful and uplifting qualities of the individual. But these qualities are not in themselves the measures for the degree of worth, nor for the limitations imposed upon the development of the individual.

A teleological analysis of the psychic differentiations of sex offers us the only possibility for arriving at a just and objective system of values for what is specifically feminine, especially with regard to restricting it in comparison with what is specifically masculine. The compulsion of woman to perform the duties of propagation places her under a natural disadvantage. For this very reason the steadily growing differentiation caused by the exaggeration of teleological peculiarities is not likely to be of service to woman. It might, indeed, appear as if the homologous development of personality according to the tendencies of primitive sex-nature ought to signify something advantageous, inasmuch as that individual being which is most thoroughly organised for the purpose of its natural calling would also prove the most efficient. But the problem is not to be solved in so simple a manner. In her ingenious and thoughtful book, *Woman and Economics*, Charlotte Perkins contends that the co-operation of erotic and economic movements in the course of civilisation's development has excessively increased all teleological sex-differentiations, so that man, in comparison with the animals, is now "over-sexed"—that is to say, the functions devoted to propagation have been forced beyond their natural confines.

But it is only when we consider the relation of the sexes to the after-generations that we are able to realise how great is the significance of this sexual intensification as a restriction laid upon the intellect of woman in comparison with that of man. It is then that the teleological sex-differentiation of the woman is heightened and increased by many various means of suggestion, religious, social and domestic. The quality of motherliness is given the highest rank among those specifically feminine characteristics which are approved by society and the mere weakening of its basic instinct is regarded as a symptom of degeneration. On the other hand, the quality of fatherliness in the man is promoted neither by education nor by common opinion, and even the entire absence of the instinct that underlies it is not regarded as anything degrading to the individual. The quality of fatherliness in man does not fall within the realm of elemental sex nature, but stands in a certain opposition to the teleological instincts of masculinity, inasmuch as it makes man equal to woman under the strain of compulsion. Apart from the close physical relationship which unites the child with its mother during the first period of its existence, there is nothing which, so far as feeling goes, distinguishes the quality of fatherliness from that of motherliness. Fatherliness is, in fact, nothing more than the masculine form of motherliness.

But for the very reason that this quality represents a trespass of man beyond the limits of his teleological nature, it assumes an immense importance in the history of humanity. Was it not fatherhood which set its seal upon the entire course of history? Was it not fatherhood which deprived the female sex of its social freedom and usurped unto itself dominion over the soul and body of woman? Charlotte Perkins conditions the evolution of man from a primitive state to the higher levels by the fact that " the free operation of the forces of maternity was circumscribed in woman, whereas similar forces in man were awakened and developed."

Yet the serious consequences which have overtaken the female sex under the conditions of modern life have not arisen merely as a result of the exaggeration of the specific sexual character, but from sex itself. Under these conditions even the honourable and highly-revered aspects of the essentially feminine nature suffer serious disadvantages; and if one regards the other side of this nature, many and serious evils are revealed. For the same teleological peculiarities which in one direction equip woman for the duties of propagation—the weakness of will which subjects itself without resistance to external influences, the intellectual inferiority which is unable to cope with anything beyond what is communicable through the senses, the preponderance of a vegetative life in a spiritual-corporeal constitution—in short, everything which may be summed up in the conception of feminine passivity—it is these very qualities which in another direction bring woman to the state in which she remains a mere tool of sex, serving the lowest masculine instincts. In other words, the bright side of the teleological sex nature disposes woman to maternity, the shadow side of the same nature—to prostitution.

The instinct of exclusive surrender to a single man which is so often described as one of the "basic instincts" of the feminine soul, is really a cultivated product—the result of a greater differentiation of woman. It has no place in the domain of her primitive sex-nature. For the exclusiveness of the surrender implies, among other things, an act of the moral will, a personal power of resistance against inner and outer temptations which at once lifts the female far above the passivity and weakness of her teleological sex-nature. Without the possession of characteristics which are more positive and therefore more "masculine" than those which originate only in the psycho-sexual disposition of primitive womanhood—sexual integrity as a voluntary moral function is unthinkable.

The fact that the tendency of primitive womanhood towards promiscuity in the sexual relationship is considered as infamous in the civilisation of western lands, bringing about the deepest degradation of the individual, is only a proof that, no matter in what degree hypocrisy and falsehood may come into play, woman as a mere elemental being can no longer exist honourably under the moral standards of such a civilisation. On the

hypothesis of the primitive life this tendency of womanhood is judged from quite another point of view, for
it is well known that many non-European peoples,
among them even those who, like the Japanese, have
achieved a high degree of culture, differ essentially in
this matter from the Europeans. Even in the pre-
Christian days of civilised European nations one encounters customs, like that of prostitution as an act
of hospitality, which indicate a conception of morality
differing greatly from the modern point of view. The
hidden relation which exists between the highest, most
honoured attribute of woman—her adaptation for
motherhood—and her most dishonourable one, par-
takes, therefore, of something monstrous only in that
estimation of woman which is held by western nations.
This relation appears still more plainly wherever the
emotions have remained more primeval, and it emerges
fully revealed in those levels of folk morality in which
motherhood is still unseparated from sexual promiscuity
and primitive womanhood has assumed the reins of
power in the shape of a Matriarchate.

The advance of civilisation distinguishes the tendencies of primitive womanhood by contrasts ever more
sharply marked, and yet in no way annuls the influences
which, under unfavourable circumstances, originate in
the teleological feminine nature. When the protection
afforded by external circumstances does not step in
as a preventive measure, then those women who in
an atavistic degree still happen to be under the influence
of the teleological weakness of their sex, must, according
to the demands of modern social laws, fall into a manner
of life which exposes them to all the lawless despotism
of masculine sexuality. Assuming that the primitive

nature of the urging which drives the unprotected creature into prostitution may be stigmatised as a symptom of degeneracy, as Lombroso holds, it nevertheless constitutes a terrible threat for those members of the female sex in whom an inner weakness is accompanied by an economic precariousness of the external means of existence.

It is in the social factor of prostitution that the teleological libidiousness of masculinity in its relation to the teleological weakness of femininity appears with all the cruel relentlessness that rages in elemental nature when the strong wage war against the feeble. And the prevailing morality which pardons the man while laying the entire burden of guilt upon the woman is here plainly shown to be nothing more than a sanctioning of this war. Man, of course, as a mere elemental being, is not to be held responsible for the constitution of a sexual nature in which the irresistible and the unconstrained elements represent a teleological operation— but only when this very sex-nature is urged as a capacity in the male sex for developing a higher spiritual morality than is possible for the female!

A state of society which so deeply degrades woman on account of a mere essential feminine weakness, should not venture upon a propaganda in which the unlimited development of the specific sex-character is advocated as a principle of evolution for woman. It would prove necessary to pay close attention not only to the protected woman, and to the so-called " noble womanhood," but also to the female sex as a whole with all the idiosyncrasies which attach to its primitive nature and social position and furnish such strong and unfortunate evidences of its teleological weakness. It is a fatal error on the part of women of the favoured classes to fancy that they are entirely free of the stigma which is inflicted upon the abandoned classes. In reality, neither their social position nor their individual lives remain uninfluenced thereby, and the dark sides of teleological womanliness avenge themselves no less upon those who are supposed to be dedicated only to the worship of its brighter side.

"Woman" is a Janus-headed creature: one face distorted by the deepest degradation with which civilisation could pollute a human being, the other face shining with the loftiest dignity with which the human race rewards the fulfilment of its heaviest duties.

But let us also inspect this face a little more closely. As a mother, woman enjoys the most ecstatic veneration: before this awe-inspiring and moving figure all the powers of life bend low in order to offer her a crown. This strain, at least, echoes in all its endless variations from every nook and corner of that world which lies poised above the real world in clouds of sentiment and beautiful thoughts. In the real world woman as a mother is somewhat less happily situated. Not only the unmarried mother—and it is only necessary to summon up this sad and dishonoured figure in order to lay bare the whole hollow phraseology of the conventional glorification of motherhood—but even the accredited mother, even she who is distinguished by many social honours, pays dearly for her maternity. The price which is paid is nothing less than spiritual freedom and equality of birth, and the farther humanity advances toward higher forms, just so much farther must the female sex, for the sake of motherhood, remain behind the male.

The teleological peculiarities which dispose woman
to motherhood create at the same time an impediment
to her mental development. It is vain to endeavour to
override this point by declaring that the education of
children, which in itself forms an integral part of
motherhood, makes lofty demands upon the psychic and
intellectual nature of the maternal woman. The modern
arrangements for education which form part of a
differentiated and cultured social order, have nothing in
common with the provisions made by nature for her
purposes of propagation.

Möbius, among others, has dealt with the relations that
subsist between primitive femininity and the purposes
of propagation in his well-known treatise, in which the
teleological sex-nature is described as " the physiological
feeble-mindedness of the female." Surely the fact that
so superficial an elaboration of the question could arouse
such attention must be ascribed to the purely aggressive
nature of this term, just as the narrow-minded vindic-
tiveness of the author's attitude was responsible for the
great bitterness it produced. Moreover, should anyone
care to observe how greatly the feminine intellect may in
certain cases excel in quality that of the masculine mind,
let him read Oda Olberg's book, *Woman and Intellectualism*—a work which, incited by the brochure of
Möbius, handles these pertinent problems with a deep,
comprehensive grasp and a fine objectivity.

Möbius postulates the point of view that " the entire
nature of woman is teleologically affected only in the
slightest degree." He thus explains teleologically the
tendency to deception or falsehood which is so frequently charged against woman in her sexual attitude
towards man. Falsehood is her " natural and indis-

pensable weapon which she finds it impossible to resign," and in order to fulfil her destiny of motherhood woman must be "child-like, patient, and simple-souled." "Far-reaching force and power, phantasy and thirst for knowledge, would surely make woman restless and hinder her in her maternal ends—therefore Nature gave her these qualities in very small doses."

Nothing need be urged against this point of view: it contains a justification of female infirmity by means of the very processes of nature herself. The fact that Möbius stands in relation to this nature process as a subjective masculine personality, and as a partisan in the question, vitiates his work, but it is injured still more by the lack of a higher point of view from which he might appreciate the problems of civilisation. He conceives of woman as a mere elemental creature, and sees her only in the perspective of her maternal calling. But it is impossible in any highly developed state of society to regard man and woman as mere elemental beings unless we also regard all civilisation as futile or as a process of degeneration. For this reason the point of view assumed by Möbius is totally obscure and contradictory. On the one hand, he accuses women of hating all new things and of frequently hanging themselves like so much lead about the neck of the struggling man: "Just as animals since time immemorial do the same things over and over again, so would the human race, had there been only women, have remained in its pristine state. All progress derives from the man." But, on the other hand, he is unable to find any measure of comparison for this progress—(and what might "progress" mean, if not the advance of civilisation?)—save this same pristine state which he must really consider as the only healthy and normal condition. For he not only holds that it is one of the unavoidable functions of civilisations to produce degenerate types, such as masculine women and feminine men, but he also charges civilisation with destroying the sources of life and with bringing about the doom of the people afflicted by it, should it not be reinvigorated in time by fresh infusions of barbaric blood. That is as much as to say that all progress which derives from man is pernicious, and all the most dominant idiosyncrasies of the male which assure him his advantage over the female, a misfortune for humanity.

What has all this to do with the conceptions of a pristine state, degeneration, progress, and civilisation? What place is to be relegated to civilisation in the life of humanity, and what place must the individual assume in the problems of civilisation?

Nature—and by this term is to be understood the entire complex of the primitive life functions, as contradistinguished from the higher impulses derived from the human intellect—Nature had no other purpose in view so far as woman was concerned, than to adapt her for motherhood, even at the cost of rendering all her other capacities inferior to those of the man. Nature flung an enormous burden upon woman, inasmuch as from the moment of conception onward she placed the entire work of generation within the female organism and subordinated it for the greater part of its individual life to this one task. In this way she exercised the greatest injustice in distributing the duties of propagation between the two sexes. Indeed, so unjust is this distribution, that even in primitive times the moral sense of man found it necessary to explain it by some theory of original sin, so that the sufferings which were laid upon woman might be considered as nothing more than punishment. For this reason does Genesis in the Old Testament declare woman to be the temptress of man, and places the stern words of the following sentence in God's mouth : —

" I will greatly multiply thy sorrow and thy conception : in sorrow thou shalt bring forth children, and thy desire shall be to thy husband, and he shall rule over thee."

And this idea has taken root so permanently that even in the middle of the nineteenth century, when attempts were first made in England to use anæsthetics in cases of painful births, the English Church protested against it as a suspension and amelioration of a divinely-decreed punishment!

The moral mania which would account for the misery of human existence by the supposition of an inherent sin has cost woman more dearly than man, for he has added guilt to her misfortune, and instead of alleviating the natural lot of woman, has merely added to its severity.

Nature may have laid a heavy burden upon woman, but civilisation has increased it to an unbearable degree. The predisposition to disease of all sorts, the diminution of resistance in the physique, the bodily softening which follows in the path of civilisation, exact a heavier penalty from the female organism than the male, because the undisturbed operation of the processes of gestation necessitates complete and perfect health. Every decrease in the physical powers of endurance in the race injures the female organism in its capacity as an instrument of propagation, and the more refined the manner of life

so much the more difficult are the duties of motherhood.

However evil the damaging influences of civilisation
may be with regard to physical qualities, the moral
values which have arisen in the track of civilisation are
still more fatal to woman as a personality. Civilisation
makes of man a twofold being whose intellectual duties
attain to a higher rank than his natural duties. It likewise differentiates individuals according to another
principle than that of genus, which decrees woman to
be the mother and man the begetter and also the supporter and defender of the family. Inasmuch as to the
duties of generation it opposes the duties of personality,
civilisation brings about a rift in the nature of the human
being and separates his consciousness into two spheres
of interest; spheres which, antagonistic at many points,
are the source of deep and serious conflicts. The higher
the individual life rises in the scale of worth, and the
more complete it becomes through achievements and
indulgences of its personality, the more easily does it
lose a proportionate interest in those duties of propagation to which the woman is so much more subservient
than the man. And with this declines also the value
which woman as such possesses in a state of civilised
society.

Civilisation being almost entirely a product of man,
shows in such results as these that it is based chiefly
upon his own needs and requirements. In primitive
conditions motherhood forms no bar nor hindrance to
the woman in any direction. Whether a gynecocratic
interpretation of " primal society " be considered as
proved or not, the fact remains that the simple division
of labour between the sexes gives to the female the same

Civilization.

rank and value as the male—the same condition exists, likewise, among those relations of man, the higher mammals. It is only under the exactions of civilisation that woman is doomed, because of her maternity, to occupy the position of a subordinate and dependent creature, a human being of the second order. The greater freedom of action which man by nature enjoys takes advantage of the sexual bondage of the woman, and thus gives to him his mastership in civilised society.

But that is in no wise to be considered as an objection to civilisation in itself. As little as the frequently observed decay of civilised peoples can be ascribed to the influence of civilisation rather than to the laws of life which manifest themselves in the birth, ripening and decay of all things, just so little is there in the nature of civilisation to decree that it should offer the woman a lesser chance of development. The one-sidedness and imperfection of all the systems of civilisation reflect only the shortcomings of the human intellect, which, as a growing and developing thing, is unable to create fitting and perfect forms or systems in which to work out its destiny. It is part of the teleological sex-nature which assures such an advantage to man over woman that it should be he who first appears as the culture-creating element. It is only where civilisation has attained to a lofty level, and the consequences of certain influences of culture have reached their full development in man, that there presents itself to woman any possibility of taking part in the work of civilisation beyond the family circle and thus obviating the one-sidedness of masculine culture.

But even with the limitations which this masculine culture has imposed upon the female sex, its mission has never been so narrowly restricted as is now demanded by those modern anti-feminists who would confine woman entirely to the duties of motherhood. They overlook the fact that the limiting of feminine activities to the family circle is related neither to the most primitive nor to the highest forms of woman's life. Among so-called aboriginal tribes women are burdened with a great many duties which, according to our ideas, ill accord with motherhood. They perform the heaviest labour, the very labours, in fact, for which uncivilised manhood has neither patience nor discipline, and with these women motherhood is something merely incidental. But in the higher circles of the society of occidental countries woman has to fulfil the duties of a fine sociability and act as the representative of her rank—the life led by the fashionable woman being in no wise favourable to maternity, but from many considerations decidedly prejudicial.

Certainly, society ladies do not dedicate the greater part of their time or their life's interests to their children. It is almost inevitable in an upper-class household that the education of children should be left to paid assistants, and those women who stand highest in the rank of cultured European society are not even permitted to suckle their children.

Even the assumption that the highest destiny of woman lies in motherhood is refuted by the history of civilisation. The moral precepts of different nations have at all times given particular importance to the renunciation of motherhood under certain circumstances, and the high value set upon virginity in the service of religious representations proves plainly enough that human society granted to certain women another voca-

tion than the so-called natural one. Even in antique
civilisations those intermediaries between the profane
world and the divine, the priests, were, so far as concerned the women who took part, bound in many ways
to the preservation of virginity. Even in Rome, where
motherhood was certainly accorded the highest rever-
ence, the vestals—women who were denied motherhood
for the sake of a higher mission—enjoyed the greatest
civic honours. Certain forms of Greek and Roman
temple-worship seem to be based upon the idea that the
economy of human society was not able to bestow
motherhood upon all women, for which reason even
those women—(usually considered everywhere as the
most degraded and degenerate)—who, not possessing the
will to motherhood, nevertheless placed themselves in
the service of sex—were to be rehabilitated by certain
religious observances.

Even in the world of Christianity, in which, as we
are aware, motherhood and virginity have been fused
into a single mystery, and one of whose direct precepts
is Paul's saying that woman would "become blessed
through the bearing of children," virginity triumphed—
virginity which, in real life, could never be united with
maternity. A vast number of the most excellent women
devoted to the spiritual Christian life have preferred
virginity to motherhood. For the religious perceptions
of the Middle Ages regarded the state of celibacy as the
only one suitable for the higher spirituality. Religiously inclined women, like religiously inclined men,
sought to prepare themselves through refuge in cloisters
for that eternal life which, beyond all considerations of
male or female, and undamaged by decrees which indicated that the way to blessedness lay in the begetting of

Motherhood & intellectual pursuit

children, offered to each sex the same state of pure spiritual felicity.

And even to-day there are countless numbers of women who, for the sake of this promised heaven, withdraw themselves into cloisters and resign all hopes of motherhood, without in any way being considered as socially inferior or as degenerate examples of womanhood.

There can, therefore, be no reason why women who, for the sake of intellectual interests, choose to forgo motherhood, should be covered with reproach. Only an age like the present, which no longer possesses a spiritual guidance, or ideals, would consider the avoidance of maternity as an objection to the intellectual endeavours of certain women.

Moreover, there is no necessity for an absolute renunciation of this function. Motherhood and intellectual labour do not mutually exclude each other; they merely create more difficult conditions in the life of the individual. Is it necessary first to prove that motherhood in itself, the bearing, bringing forth, and rearing of children, makes heavy physical and psychical demands upon the individual, and that these demands increase in direct proportion with the number of children? But as evidence of how even the most obvious truths have become questionable, it is only necessary to point to books, such as those written by Adele Gerhardt and Helene Simon, in which an elaborate investigation is made, to ascertain "whether motherhood and intellectual work" hinder each other, and in what way.

If it were true—as has been tirelessly affirmed by whole schools of sociologists ever since the days of Rousseau—that it is the duty of every woman to be constantly pregnant because the "genius of the race" demands this (Sombart), then, to be sure, there would be no possibility of uniting motherhood and intellectual work, for the complete using-up of feminine fertility permits of no participation in other activities.

But, having regard to the difficult and complicated conditions which lie at the root of the problem of population, such decisions, valid only for the simplest, most primitive forms of society, will hardly suffice. The right of the individual deliberately to limit the number of offspring cannot, as a matter of principle, be disputed, even though it may remain an open question whether the declaration of Malthus that it is even a sacred duty of that individual, be justifiable. As a moral problem the only question is whether there be any moral difference between the means of restriction employed—that is to say, between abstinence and prevention.

Nature herself who, through elemental means, furthers the human increase, also provides the elemental means for the necessary restriction. Even in the midst of civilisation there exist conditions which betray the fact that the virtual capacity for increase is subject to the same laws which limit it in the realm of primitive nature. Among these conditions—if we exclude war as an abnormal contingency—we may first cite the enormous infant mortality among the lower classes, or the involuntary celibacy of unmarried women—whose numbers in Germany alone amount to some two millions. But more potent than all other factors in a pseudo-monogamous state of society such as that of modern civilised nations, does the factor of prostitution operate to limit the natural increase in the population.

It may safely be left for the moralists to decide which

"Restriction of off-spring":

manner of restriction may be called the most pernicious, but why should the compensating factor of an increase in population, hindered as it is by so many other influences, be exacted only from married women?

If the history of mankind is to instruct us further, the deliberate restriction of offspring is a phenomenon which necessarily begins to manifest itself as soon as the density of population in relation to the means of subsistence has reached a certain height—whether the means of prevention are such as are in use among occidental peoples, or whether the barbaric method of exposing and slaying infants prevails, as in the Orient.

Those rigorous extremists who defend the cause of propagation, and insist on a complete exhaustion of the fertility of married women, frequently charge certain features of the woman's movement with being responsible for the growing disinclination of cultured women to bear an unrestricted number of children. He who believes that the slight influences which these features have hitherto exerted could produce such far-reaching results, should devote himself to a study of France, where the increase in population was commonly known to have come to a standstill long before the first sign of a French feminist movement made itself visible. Moreover, what short-sightedness it is to hold only the female portion of the population responsible for the causes of this standstill! In that respect the astute originators of the Code Napoleon had a far deeper glimpse into the verity of things when they framed that regulation which, unmerciful as it may have been with regard to the teleological weakness of the female, nevertheless aided the cause of procreation, even if in an illegitimate way: *la recherche de la paternité est interdite.*

The woman's movement and the disinclination for an unrestricted number of children are phenomena which are coincident in time, but do not stand in relation to each other as cause and effect. It is possible that one may be able to trace some connection between them in the profounder basic strata of the social structure in which they appear. Primitive communities, which are predominantly warlike and show an inordinate consumption of human lives, must make use of the fertility of their women to the fullest extent. Highly cultivated, and for that reason peace-loving communities, grant a longer average measure of life to their members. The renewal of the generations need not take place so rapidly, and the single individual whose cultivation takes so much longer, and is so much more tedious and costly than is the case in primitive conditions, represents a being of superior worth. It is, therefore, a necessary consequence of culture that the unrestricted functioning of motherhood is no longer regarded by the social consciousness as of the same incomparable importance. And it appears to be equally inevitable that the number of women who can devote themselves to the function must decline in the same proportion as the external and internal conditions of existence become more and more complicated for the individual.

A woman who is to fulfil her destiny may dedicate herself either to producing a numerous family or to following a profession. But should she decide to burden herself with neither, then the value of her life must decline in comparison with the achievements which represented a woman's life in earlier epochs of civilisation—(for to have borne and raised ten or twelve children, and, in addition to this, to have conducted a

household under the former primitive conditions of production—that certainly was an accomplishment excelled
by very few!)—although the value of such a woman's
life sinks still farther when compared with the tasks
accomplished by man.

Such is the fate of the middle-class women of the
present. Only a very few of the professions are open
to them, and the exercise of all activity outside the
circle of the family is rendered extremely difficult for
them as soon as they seek to combine it with the
"natural" calling of woman. Whosoever would attempt to persuade such women to an acceptance of un-
controlled motherhood, or endeavour to hold up to them
the life-work of women of an earlier period as a model,
cannot be aware of the deep-lying causes of the changes
with which the civilisation of the present day is indis-
solubly bound up. And when, as present evidence
shows, there is an attempt to introduce laws making
marriage impossible for those women who occupy public
positions, or even directly to forbid them to enter the
marriage state, then one merely takes away with one
hand that which one exacts with the other, and adds,
officially, another factor to those which are already at
work in the restriction of the population.

The tendencies of the woman's movement have also
been attacked as conducive to degeneration, inasmuch
as they alienated woman from her proper vocation and
filled her with an intellectual pride and ambition prejudicial to her mission as a mother. The fact has been
overlooked that it is precisely the woman's movement
which acts as a palliative to the dangers of degeneration
caused by the indolence of those women of the wealthier
classes whose original sphere of labour has been lost in

a social order that has not provided them with any equivalent in the work of society.

The numerical superiority of a race is always guaranteed by broader and more stable classes of the people than those which represent intellect and culture. For this reason the well-known antithesis which exists between mental and physical productivity can in no wise furnish an excuse for excluding women of this class from participation in the intellectual interests which distinguish their men. But the fear that women devoting themselves to intellectual work will entirely lose their predisposition for child-bearing is quite stupid and unnecessary. On the contrary, motherhood furnishes a guaranty that the intellectualism of women will never plunge them into that ill-balanced relationship with the natural and elemental things of life so frequently to be observed among men of intellect. <u>Nature has implanted the maternal instinct so deeply that it is not easily to be uprooted at the option of any individual</u>—more than that, she has surrounded the quality of motherhood with so lofty a sanctity that every female heart not utterly withered away is irresistibly attracted by it.

When, in spite of all this, individual women voluntarily surrender motherhood for the sake of devoting themselves to some intellectual aim in life, there should be excellent reasons for regarding this as due to an heroic feminine sentiment. In the struggle of a personality against tradition in order to give play to the higher motives of the will of that personality—a will which in tragic instances is not dismayed even by death —there lies a wholly heroic element, and only the dullest utilitarianism would presume, when estimating the social value of the individual woman, to ignore those equivalents which she offers to mankind for her renunciation of progeny.

As to the conception of degeneracy, an objective view of modern feminine problems would have to take full cognisance of the fact that degeneracy and development are closely-knit phenomena not easily distinguishable among themselves. A return to an imaginary condition of primitive nature, stamping as a futile mistake the whole enormous fabric of masculine civilisation, must, like every other reversion or forcing-back, present nothing but an aspect of hopelessness. The only means capable of combating the evils which have arisen out of a high degree of civilisation, must be sought in that civilisation itself. The chief problem of all sociological endeavour is how to overcome the imperfections of the intermediate stages by a still further intensification of civilisation. It is in this sphere that we behold the changes which are to prepare those new conditions for woman under which she may be enabled to devote herself to the duties of a higher spiritual life without resigning her duties as an elemental being—conditions which will dower her with that highest triumph of all civilisation—the unhampered self-predestination of the individual.

It would be an unreasonable hope, far exceeding anything one might demand of the average masculinity, to expect to bring about these changes solely through the work and knowledge of men. The problem of obtaining a different position for women in the social order of the future is something that must be solved by women themselves. It is that which forms the greatest social mission of every woman who, by inclination and activity, has risen above the traditional sphere of her

sex.   Under the forms of society which exist to-day a
combination of maternity and intellectual work is
possible only under the greatest disadvantages.   New
divergences are to be made—and this is a task which
can be fulfilled only by those women who, in agreement
with the constitution of their souls, need not subject
themselves to the leadership of men.   The great weakness of modern civilisation with regard to the position
it has assigned to woman consists in the very fact that
it is the result of man's work, created by man for
the purposes of man, and thus unadapted to the
woman as an individual.   Under the dominance
of such one-sided interests it could not well be
otherwise.

The typical masculine, like the typical feminine, both
with regard to the family and to society, has produced
everything that, according to its general character, it was
capable of producing.   It is a fallacy to expect that in
the society of the future a new emancipation will arise
out of that specific nature of woman which is commonly
conceived as the sense of motherliness raised to the lofty
degree of an intuition for the sake of the common good.
This motherliness of the specifically feminine soul can,
according to the limitations of its nature, by no means
devote itself to the interests of the common good, for
its greatest power lies in its concentration upon its own
progeny.   The blind instinct with which every woman
prefers and exalts her own offspring is something that
is teleologically inevitable.

The social sense—that faculty which, to use Christian
terminology, is called the love of one's fellow-man—
demands a higher differentiation of the individual than
is possible with the instinct of maternity—otherwise this

sense would not have first manifested itself as a peculiarity of the male sex.

Changes in the social order can be brought about only through such women as have been freed of the teleological limitations of the sex, who vary from the prevailing type, and who, through the force of their independence, attain to a new conception of life. Such women, if you choose, are the " unwomanly " ones—no doubt less useful for man and the elemental sex purpose, and yet indispensable factors of the advancing processes of civilisation.

The general mass of women should, however, be wise enough to overlook all opposite traits, and not refuse to recognise the community of interests represented by the advanced woman, for the triumphs which the latter will achieve will in the future order of things also redound to the benefit of the former.

APPENDIX:

ON THE TRAINING OF THE CHILD

There is a prevailing tendency to regard the training of the young as a special function of the mother—the father's share in the matter being forced considerably into the background; in fact, so much so that it might almost appear as if woman, by means of her physical and ethical achievements, were endeavouring in this direction to obtain a matriarchal power over posterity. It might therefore seem that the training of children, representing a far more permanent, intensive, and comprehensive demand upon the feminine personality than the physical duty of motherhood, would bind women for the greater part of their lives so closely to their families that

the advanced / "unwomanly a woman

devotion to any other profession in conjunction with this maternal duty would be absolutely precluded.   But the experiences of everyday life, prove, nevertheless, that there are women who, in addition to a large flock of children, find time and interest for many other personal activities—and also others whose attention is so absorbed by the care of a single child that they are lost to the rest of the world—from which it may be seen that here, too, the individual tendency operates as the deciding factor.   And yet stronger and stronger grows the tendency to consider the problem of child-training as of such pre-eminent importance that its social value exceeds that of all other human endeavours.

The most perfect expression of these ideas is to be found in the works of Ellen Key: "The greatest faculties are necessary to do justice to even a single child. That does not mean, to be sure, that one must devote one's entire time to the child.   But it means that our souls must be possessed by the child—just as the scientist is possessed by his researches and the artist by his creations"; for the lofty task must be this, "to train the new race which will some day form a community of men in which the perfected human being— the ' Superman '—will be revealed in the rosy dawn of a still distant day."   (*The Century of the Child.*)

Here we have a combination of two modern ideas which in their essence are diametrically opposed and irreconcilable, the one being a presentation of the decisive influence of education in the life of the individual, and the other that of a new and higher race, that of the " superman."

Nietzsche, the father of the modern superman, left —no doubt intentionally—the outlines of this figure rather vague, but inasmuch as he declares in a certain passage that the goal of all development must be sought in " the sovereign individual, who alone resembles himself," one must assume that by this he meant a man who derives the impulses of his acts from himself, and, independent of the influences of his environment, develops himself into a self-governing personality—a man who is his own creation.

To individualities of such tendencies education has but little to offer. In order that a man might grow to be entirely himself, he must first of all completely conquer the influences of his environment and his education. He must overcome the best as well as the worst influences—unless a good education is to mean nothing more than good breeding—an automatic command of external forms.

And what more, indeed, should one expect of the training of the young? Even the commonly accepted formula that such training should develop good tendencies, and obliterate the bad, is totally inadequate. Bearing in mind the uncertainty with which one must regard what is good and what evil in the constitution of a human soul—for every person must possess the faults of his merits, regarding these quite apart from customary moral values—it is only too probable that a pedagogic choice between the good and the bad would not always separate the wheat from the chaff. In addition to this, every system of education which aspires to be something more than a mere education of outward forms, must assume that there exists a wide and intuitive sympathy on the part of the instructors towards the instructed, and such an intuition is to be found only in a superior personality. Those parents who would attain to such an intuitive understanding of their children must not be possessed of offspring who would rise above them in the matter of intellect. It would be impossible for such children to be "new men or women," for how would ordinary human beings be able to train the extraordinary? According to all probabilities, ordinary parents would produce ordinary children. When human beings of the average sort intermarry, then it might safely be foretold that the children of such a union will also be average human beings, despite all strenuous attempts at training. Should it, however, by chance occur that a wonderful, unconjectured stranger, a genius, should make his appearance among them, then the best thing his progenitors can do is to let him go his own ways, without oppressing him with their pedagogic arts.

Considered in an active sense, education may be held to be the expression of a sort of *being*—that is, one educates with what one is, rather than with what one knows. No pedagogic knowledge, nor intention, however great, will make a good instructor out of an unsuitable personality. The stipulation that we must first train ourselves ere we can train others offers no solution for this difficulty. For this presupposes a distinct faculty which is not possessed by everyone, namely, the faculty of educating oneself. And if it is at all possible to educate oneself, then the parents might as well leave this to the children themselves. Is not that man who has been able to educate himself to be considered superior to him who has permitted this to be performed for him by others?

At the most it might be said that the average human being will always be subject to such training, good or bad, and especially those feeble individuals who, incapable of standing alone, succumb most easily to the suggestive influences of the prevailing norm. The use, significance, and purpose of education can therefore never be identified with the creation of a " new " race, nor even of the " superman," but must merely serve as protection and guidance for the less capable and resistant elements.

But even with regard to these, the old parallel which compares the training of a child with the creation of a work will no longer hold good. Women are particularly fond of consoling themselves for their lack of partici- pation in intellectual things—a lack imposed upon them by motherhood—by having recourse to this comparison. It is the old cry: women themselves should be nothing and do nothing, but should rather endeavour to foster or create in their sons that which they themselves are denied the right of being.

Among all the false, rudimentary ideas in which the ethics of the bourgeoisie are so fertile, there could scarcely be found another so pernicious as this. For it is just this which leads to those abuses of a pedagogy conscious of its goal, and notoriously evil in its effects, and it prepares the bitterest disappointments for the *naïve* souls of those women who build their life-work upon it. Despite all the arts of education—who, indeed, can doubt it?—a man remains what he was born; a tiny ego will not grow into a greater even under the stimulus of the most fervent motherly self-sacrifice, nor an or- dinary intelligence become a genius. The woman who omits to develop any special talent of her own because of her belief that it is possible for her to " develop " it in her son, will, in ninety-nine cases out of a hundred, be grievously cheated of the fruits of her life. Why not

live your own lives, dear mothers, and thereby spare
your children all these immense burdens of hopes
and wishes which they must bear with them under the
supposition that their duty in life is to please you and
not themselves!

It is rather the exception than the rule to find children
so similar to the parents that a full understanding is
possible between them.   Every generation develops
itself in certain opposite ways to the one preceding it;
the parent-generation uses up the spiritual possessions
whose bearer it had been, the child-generation must
create new ones for itself.   In that consists its spiritual
life-function, and should it limit itself to retaining the
ideals of good education which have been delivered to
it, it would give away its most precious privilege.

Biologically, too, the child is but seldom a continua-
tion or image of its parents.   Biological development,
like that of civilisation itself, does not progress in a
straight line.   The mother and father are mere intermediate members—the child itself comes from a far
greater distance; it is, at least, in an equal degree the
child of unknown ancestors as that of the two individuals
who have come together for its begetting.

The belief of parents that they themselves may live
again in their children belongs to those illusions by
means of which nature renders the demands she makes
in behalf of propagation agreeable to the individual
consciousness.   Even though the mere generative life
be accompanied by such deceptive phenomena, the
realm of reason, at least, ought to remain free of them.
But a similar misleading illusion arises even here
through the notion that the child is the " work " of its
parents, especially of the mother who trains it.   Who-

ever regards motherhood as the equivalent of intellectual productivity, overlooks the fact that a work is the achievement of a personality, but not so a child. There is, to be sure, a certain idea common to both cases, by means of which the individual justifies to himself all the great personal efforts and sacrifices which he has made for the sake of his work. Such is the idea of living again in after ages, of stretching his own destiny over a period of time that is immeasurably prolonged. But any farther comparison between the two is possible only through an erroneous interpretation of the function of education.

The relation of the parents to the children, when based merely upon the generative life, is in the highest degree irrational. Should one attempt to explain and justify it by means of the reason, that would be possible only from a primitive-natural point of view—that is to say, from the position which man occupies as a mere elemental being. The idea of personality, with all the complexity of feelings and strivings which are part of it, could not be utilised for this purpose. In the same degree in which woman is a personality, will she make demands outside of her maternal sphere for an independent participation in the matters of life. The conflict with her duties as an elemental being which thereupon ensues cannot be disposed of by a deliberate confusion of the elements of personality with those of the species.

This confusion will occur but seldom in the case of a man, even though the primitive male, whose life-work consists in the preservation of a very numerous progeny, must certainly be conceived as being burdened more heavily by the demands of the species than, say, a

excesses of motherhood

wealthy lady who has merely to bring up two or three children. Let it be assumed, however, that this confusion is in the nature of an intellectual license in favour of the highest conceivable development of the sense of maternity—there could be, nevertheless, nothing more dangerous for the freedom of the children and their personal development than the tendency of a mother to regard her offspring as her work, and to consider their bringing-up as the one single duty of her life. This inclination to drive motherhood to excess is frequently a source of danger for the growing children, especially in the life of large modern cities, where household duties make such slight demands on women. And this is still more pertinent when we remember that the small families of to-day are not regulated as were formerly the large families, in which the great number of children made necessary a division of the maternal duties among so many persons that any single child was safe from being disturbed and burdened with an excessive number of rules for its bringing-up. The incessant guarding, spoiling, and coddling practised by those mothers whose one occupation consists of training the young, and who are inspired by the proud ambition to leave a perfected " work " to posterity in the shape of their child, merely create useless beings, who must first undergo a stern discipline in life beyond the maternal-domestic sphere ere they are able to rid themselves of the consequences of the training they have undergone.

And, then, ought we not also to put the question : What adult person really cares to be considered as the product of the training he has received? This thought is not likely to make any person particularly elate. Nor is it calculated to arouse the gratitude of children; on the contrary, all too easily it inspires the children with a tendency to hold their parents to account for all that life has withheld from them, and even for their personal shortcomings. Gratitude towards parents can really be maintained only under the supposition that each man is the result of his own endeavours, and that he owes his parents some recompense for the pain and trouble he has caused them. For, in reality, they served only as the means of which he availed himself in order to attain to his own existence—an idea which Schopenhauer has carried out in a philosophically-phantastic manner in his *Metaphysics of Love*. But apart from all metaphysical backgrounds, and judged purely with regard to the species, parents are to be considered as intermediary links—as the soil in which the new human being is to grow as a work of nature. Were it in any sense true that a man is the work of his parents, we would certainly have so great a cause for dissatisfaction with the bungling processes to which we have been subjected, that feelings of gratitude would never arise.

Again, no thinking and conscientious man would, under a supposition such as this, venture to bring a new being into the world and endeavour to educate it. To insist upon the responsibility towards one's own descendants as being a personal obligation might serve the purpose of inducing sick persons, or those afflicted with hereditary or acquired defects, to resign their hopes of possessing progeny. Nevertheless, considering the vast spread of inherited deficiencies and evils, and the uncertainty that attends all the regulative forces that operate against heredity—forces in which lies the entire vitality of a race—even this appears questionable. Rather than afflict the consciousness of civilised man with so deep a burden of pessimism, all social endeavour ought to be bent toward first abolishing the evils under which the individual sinks, and then to destroying the influences which in the shape of social conditions tend to foster degeneration.

And here, too, we touch upon the problem of training the child. Far more decisively than the most comprehensive provisions of an individualistic training, do the external conditions of life operate upon the young man. But this truth, so unpleasant to contemplate, is the very one which mothers most stubbornly refuse to accept. Otherwise every woman who has the destiny of her children seriously at heart would despair at the helplessness in which, for instance, she stands in relation to her fifteen-, sixteen-year-old sons as soon as the world, in the abominable shape which sexual things have assumed under the dominance of men, begins to absorb them. Could only those women who persist in holding fast to the old standard of motherhood learn to know that they need not yet for a considerable time abandon this standard in order to feel that it is their duty to take part in social work.

But when one observes the indifference and stupidity with which women who dedicate their entire lives to the cause of education, overlook the conditions into which their male children are plunged when scarcely full-grown, then one is moved to ask whether the entire chauvinism of education does not merely serve as an excuse for glossing over the lives of women with an appearance of more worth and substance than they really deserve at the present stage of civilisation.

It might, of course, seem that we are moving in a circle when we ignore the influences of education in order to devote our entire energies to the conditions of social life. A new order of things can be created only by people who, because they are possessed of other needs and sentiments, find the old order unendurable. Is it, therefore, not absolutely indispensable to implant these needs and sentiments in their souls from their earliest years on? But whoever would aspire to implant anything new must first of all prove himself to be regenerated. And with this we arrive once more at the starting-point: regenerated human beings are born, not bred; they are a work of nature, and not of their parents.

Every age has its peculiar superstitions. The superstition with respect to the power and influence of education is quite particularly the superstition of an age whose knowledge of the meaning of the world reaches its extreme height in the concept of evolution. An everlasting *becoming* without a consummated *being*, a future which constantly converts itself into an empty present, can never satisfy the human longing to know the meaning and purpose of life. If life really unrolls itself as an eternal alternation of the generations of which the individuals are only mere transitory links without an individual content, then the prospects for an unlimited development become as naught. That which is can never mean less than that which is to be. This axiom is a valid one for man—should it not also properly serve for woman? To sink their entire personality in motherhood, or in the training of the young, as some would like to prescribe, even for those women who are capable of other things, is to sacrifice the certain to the possible, the thing that is to the thing that might be. With an expansion of mother-love such as this, one undertakes, to quote the words of Malwida von Meysenbug, "the sacrifice of oneself; that is to say, the sacrifice of that which no one is permitted to sacrifice."

THE TYRANNY OF THE NORM

IT is undeniable that there are many women who go far beyond the feminine average in regard to intellect and strength of character, and many who are well qualified for careers and occupations other than those customary to the sex. There are many—but are there enough?

It is possible that the woman thus exceptionally endowed might be found to be so rare a phenomenon as to count for very little in the economy of society. It is possible that she might be discounted as merely a transient exception, without influence upon the institutions of the social commonwealth. At all periods of the world's history there have been women who have equalled or even excelled the majority of men in intelligence and in energy; yet they have not been able to alter the social position of their sex either in the matter of the law or in regard to standards of opinion. They have been exceptions and have been treated as such. They were exceptions—that is to say, they were not specimens of a new line of development; they were not pioneers opening out new routes for a future generation to follow and develop; they had no successors.

Therein lies the difference between the isolated feminine individualities of earlier epochs and the

leaders of the modern woman's movement. The latter
are not satisfied to be what they are and to enjoy alone
the positions which in all circumstances may be conquered by powerful personalities. They seek to adapt
existing social conditions to their nature and needs, and
to transform the prevailing idea of what women should
be in the interests of those women who vary from the
norm—the accepted type.

In this consists the great importance of the woman's
movement—its claim to be regarded as a social reforma-
tion. But, so far as lasting results are concerned, its
efficiency will be dependent upon the degree to which
the sex in general can be won over to it. All social
forms, habits, customs, traditions, may be traced back to
a majority; and standards of opinion, accepted views of
life, are but indices to the average type represented by
humanity of a certain epoch. By means of these the exceptional individual finds his exceptional needs opposed
to those of the majority. In so far as he differs from his
fellows, he must either oppose his will to theirs or else,
if his personality be not strong enough for that, subordinate himself to them, however unwillingly.

This battle between the normal majority and the
individual deviating from the norm and striving to break
down its tyranny, goes deep down into the constitution
of society; and the process involved is nothing less than
the organic evolution of civilisation.

It is possible to class human beings in two opposed
groups according to their intellectual tendencies—a
broad classification, of course, in which the gradations
are ignored. They correspond with the tendencies to
conserve and to renew, which, according to the Darwinian theory, are the determining forces in the evolu-

tion of species. The great psychologist Maudsley has compared them with the fundamental cosmic laws of the universe. Human thought, he tells us, is ruled as much by antagonistic forces as is the course of the planets. A centrifugal or revolutionary force gives the expansive impulse to new ideas, while a centripetal or conservative force tends to keep them from changing; and the resultant from these two opposing forces is the direction in which intellectual evolution progresses.

The stationary element in intellectual life is represented by that majority which looks upon inherited standards as irrevocable, upon the old truths as sacred and eternal, whether regarded as divine ordinances or as the expression of an accepted code of morality to which all must conform.

The moving element, the element of change and development, is, however, represented by single and exceptional individualities. Individuality is the source whence spring all the new forms of knowledge, all the new needs, all the new possibilities of existence. It is in this that Nature manifests herself most fully and clearly, for here its original essence is not effaced or disguised by external rules, such as those of custom, tradition and the conception of duty. To bring this original essence into action as a living force in conflict with tradition, to shatter and reconstruct atrophied forms of life through the force of a revolutionary movement— that must constitute its mission in the social commonwealth.

Human beings of the centrifugal or progressive order of mind envisage life differently from those of conservative temperament. The thought that they are pioneers, that they have set foot in the unknown, that they have risks and perils to cope with, affords them the same moral satisfaction that the man of conservative tempera-- ment derives from behaving correctly and carrying out the duties prescribed for him. They will have nothing to do with external rules, they will not obey the tradi- tional code of laws, but will listen only to the behests of their own nature.

The destiny of such innovators varies according to the force of their personality, irrespective of whatever field of intellectual activity to which they may belong. They may be merely ridiculed or ignored, they may be misunderstood or persecuted, their end may be misery, insanity, or a martyr's death. Such men are in truth martyrs in the cause of humanity. To them we owe every forward step in the progress of the race from the condition of beasts up to the noblest and loftiest civilisation. And when a people ceases to produce such individuals, it sinks into petrification or stagnancy; its power of development dies away.

Thus, with the irresistible force of a natural law, this conflict between the two opposing tendencies is eternally waged. So long as the revolutionary individual stands alone, he is outlawed; it is only when he acquires a following, an adequate number of sympathisers and supporters, that accepted ideas begin to give way before him.

In the intellectual movement of the nineteenth century this conflict found its most conspicuous expression in the battle over what was styled "Free Thought." In Germany the opponents of "Free Thought," or of "Free Spirits," came to be styled "Philistines," a term chiefly familiar until then as applied by the University student to those whose narrow, bourgeois views and

Philistines.

habits of life contrasted with his own joyous and un-restricted outlook. Later the term was adopted by prominent thinkers to characterise the mob that showed itself hostile to their ideas. Wagner denounced as Philistines all who were lacking in artistic sensibility. Schopenhauer used the word in speaking of men devoid of spiritual needs. He attributed this lack to "the strict and closely normal measure of their intellectual powers." Lombroso described aversion from the new as "Misoneismus," and spoke of it as a distinguishing characteristic of the normal, respectable man. He held that in so far as an individual being was progressive, so far is he removed from the normal, for the average measure of human intelligence is not sufficient to permit of progress beyond the accepted type nor of the conception of new ideas.

Those forces which in Germany were called Philistine have taken a particularly strong stand against the feminist movement. And this not merely in work-a-day life. In no department of literature have the uncritical exponents of accepted ideas gone more widely astray than in their discussion of "Woman." Most of their theses are directed rather towards setting forth the general conditions fitted for woman and recording the recognised spiritual differences between the sexes than towards allotting due scope to individuality. Their aim was not to make provision for all the endless varieties of individual needs, but to devise a formula according to which the needs of the individual should be brought into harmony with her sex and by which her position in society should be clearly fixed. It will be observed that with people of conservative tendency the need of accepted standards of thought and conduct is greater than the need of objective perception; and it happens only too often, even with the most untrammelled minds, that they do not distinguish between their personal emotions and their critical judgment. Many distinguished men whose intellectual bent is altogether in the direction of free thought are reactionaries in regard to women. The reason for this is to be found in the constitution of a certain species of masculinity: it is the sexual element in them that brings about the misuse of their intellectual faculties.

The progressive individual, in the case of a woman, has therefore a twofold struggle with conformity: she has to contend with the accepted type which the ruling masculine notion has set up for womanhood, and also with the actual predominating womanly type which stands for the average of the sex as it is at the moment. She is appraised not according to her own characteristics, but according to the normal characteristics of her sex, and not even as they really are, but as they appear on the surface. If at present the opposition to this method of generalisation (to which the individual man is subject as much as the individual woman) happens to manifest itself chiefly among the female sex, it is not to be attributed merely to the fact that the normative type among men already entitles them to all the liberties and advantages of their class in the State and society of to-day. This type may be compared to a capacious coat of mail, made according to the largest size, a coat most uncomfortable for the weaker individuals, though it may not hinder the development of the stronger ones. In the case of the woman the accepted type provides far less scope for the evolution of individuality. It is primitive in its workings, like a strait-waistcoat, which the individual woman must burst asunder if she is not to be stifled.

A very widely held theory regards man as the exemplar of the progressive, centrifugal tendency, and woman as stationary and centripetal. This accords with the conception of biologists in regard to the male sex having an individualistic, revolutionary bent, individualising and renovating the race, and the female sex being by nature conservative and tending to the conservation of the race. It is indeed one of the most widely accepted of all established ideas that " woman " is the guardian of customs, the champion of things as they are, irrevocably wedded to tradition.

But it ought to be always remembered that progressiveness is characteristic of only a very small number of men and by no means of the majority of them; while in all revolutionary epochs we are confronted with the names of women who played their parts, however difficult it was for members of their sex to overcome the traditional barriers in their way.

The classical example of this tendency towards progress in the female sex is offered by those women who first introduced the feminist movement. For over a century they and their successors had to be content to be reckoned as degenerates. They were generally regarded as perverted types not to be ranked among worthy specimens of their sex. Indeed, it is not so long since they were spoken of as " men-women." It was not possible to view as other than freaks and abnormalities these creatures who came upsetting established ideas and questioning approved tenets; the new paths they sought to make for themselves could be held to be nothing but blind alleys down which the sex was being

feminist movement & its 2-fold reception:

enticed to stray from its natural sphere and its "natural destiny." Even now we may hear the voices of those who persist in regarding the entire feminist movement as a symptom of degeneration.

From the standpoint of the conservative tendency such a view of the movement is justified, though from the progressive standpoint it is regarded as something to praise, not to condemn. How any such manifestation is to strike the observer, depends entirely upon whether he belongs to the first or the second order of these men.

From the standpoint of free intellectuality, it is a reactionary proceeding to make out a table of spiritual differences between the sexes and to pin one's faith to it as to an incontrovertible dogma. For the man of untrammelled mind, such a standard is found to be at fault from the moment when superior beings who do not accord with it make their appearance; for him there are only certain criteria in accordance with which everyone may select an individual of the opposite sex suited to him and his kind, and sufficient in herself. He does not reckon it a praiseworthy thing if an individual possesses the typical qualities of his or her sex, any more than he prides himself on bearing the stamp of his social position or his professional calling. It is the essence of individuality to deviate from the typical as from the conventional. Is this to be curbed by conventional ideas in regard to sex attributes? A general rule drawn from a majority of cases has no value as applied to a single specimen; it can certainly not be taken as a criterion by which to classify the possessor of an exceptionally developed mind as "normal" or "abnormal." To appraise the individuality thus deviating from the average, one should not take up the viewpoint of the existing and accepted type; one must study it in perspective from the viewpoint of the evolution of the species, inseparable both in its tendencies to conserve and to renew. The evolution of species is unceasing, though imperceptible; every new individuality involves new possibilities of life. Nature is a spendthrift in forms of life, and the bountifulness that produces countless variations in the lower forms of life reaches its apex among the higher races of mankind in differences of personality.

The history of humanity is a record of gradual progress towards individual freedom. In primitive states of society, the individual is generally kept in submission to the interests of the community; but the higher the social organism, the richer is it in its forms of life and the more thorough its provision for the freedom of the human individual.

Even the most perfect kind of freedom would have to depend upon an exact balance between these two opposing forces of progressiveness and conservatism. To sacrifice the individual to the community is an archaic course—to hand over the community to the unfettered will of the individual, a decadent one. The conservative tendency of the majority affords a necessary and indispensable counterweight to the progressive tendency; without this it would be as impossible for the social life of humanity to go on as it would be for the universe to continue in existence without the counteraction of the force of gravitation to the rotation of the spheres. Human society would have no element of permanence and stability but for the co-operation of the centripetal order of mind. In times when the centrifugal order of mind is preponderant, in times of change and revolution, human affairs assume a restless insecure aspect; all accepted ideas are questioned, life becomes a feverish succession of changes, each new phase vanishing suddenly and completely. Tradition is the work of the conservative majority; and it is to tradition that every species of civilisation must look for the solid foundation, the organic principles, which are essential to its unity and continuity.

It is a very common failing in men of progressive intellect to ignore the nature of the ordinary run of mankind in their campaign for freedom, to brand them as narrow-minded and to overlook entirely their duty in the social order of life.

The contemptuous term of "Philistine" which in Germany is applied by the progressive to his adversary is expressive of the fact that the word is derived from the field of polemics. Ought not the free spirit to be capable of playing a non-partisan part in the sphere of intellectual discussion? Might we not refrain henceforth from using the word "Philistine," substituting in its stead the expression Normal Thinker?

The social function of the progressive mind has its origin, then, in its relation to the Normal Thinker. Freedom in its negative sense, freedom from rules and regulations, is only one of its elements, as an active force it creates new ideas, whose future is dependent upon the manner in which they are accepted and elaborated by others. It creates new "ideals"—that is to say, if we avoid the terms of the metaphysician—it lays down new lines along which the evolution of the race shall proceed.

If the negative part of freedom separates the individual from the social community, the positive part

of it draws him all the more closely into it.   In so far
as the progressive spirit is to be creative in regard to
morals and customs, in so far is it dependent upon a
public—as is the case with artistic genius.   The idea of
creating new modes of existence, of enacting new codes
of law, has always been the stimulus and prerogative of
the very great among men of progressive mind.   With
these aims in view, they probe into the nature of their
kind, into the mysteries concealed behind the process
of evolution.   They are thus the first to bring into
shape something which in subsequent generations will
have become common; they are forerunners of others—
the heralds of Nature that the species is still alive, still
in process of growth.   All the ideas that take their place
as accepted truths in the consciousness of society, the
entire structure of moral and intellectual values and all
that exercises a decisive influence in the lives of the
majority, were originally conceived in the minds of
the few.   Up to a certain point, the majority takes its
shape in accordance with the ideals of the few.   But for
this process these ideals would vanish like transient
moods and fancies with the individuals in whose minds
they were conceived.

Of course, only those things which answer to the
needs and faculties of the majority pass into the general
stock; and the process by which, when changed into
the normal, they become common property, is enacted
upon the very threshold of the social consciousness.
It is a noteworthy failing of the conservative type of
mind that it takes no account of the genesis of the
normal, and that it regards it as something fixed instead
of as it really is, something that has grown and is still
in process of change.   The binding force of the normal

lies in the need of the normal thinker to cling to it as to an infallible law, a need that can only be satisfied by the idea that he is hearkening to a higher will, not to that of a few individuals. He honours in the normal the expression of the will of society, to oppose which would mean his destruction, since he could not in himself exist alone.

If the conception of evolution, with reference to human society, is to have any significance at all, then a progressive raising of the average type is a necessary hypothesis. It is, however, impossible to believe that the great majority could ever, in the course of development, progress from the plane of accepted standards to that of untrammelled intellectuality. Assuming the mental productiveness, a free spirit is inherent like any other talent. For even those free personalities whose mental significance does not extend beyond their own private spheres are productive in so far as that the intuitions which govern their actions and judgments are evolved from within themselves. The qualities, therefore, which will never overflow from the plane of progressive intellectuality into that of the accepted standards, which can never become " normal," are the fundamental instincts and the entire mode of thought connected with them. It is the right of the strong to fashion life according to their inclination, but this cannot become the maxim of the weak, and therefore not of the majority.

Nietzsche refers to the relation between the progressive and the conservative intellect when he says: " It would be altogether unworthy of a great mind to see an objection in mediocrity, *per se*. Mediocrity itself is the primary cause of the necessity for exceptions: it demands a higher development." And he indicates the legislative mission of the master mind in Zarathustra's words : "Be firm, my friends; for your hand shall be laid upon thousands of years "—whilst Max Stirner, so closely connected with him in thought, has carried the war against all mediocre endeavours to their final, logical annihilation. Max Stirner's work is, it is true, a triumph of abstract thought, the most absolute expression of centrifugal intellectuality, but it is ineffectual so far as the actual conditions of human social life are concerned.

So long as the feminist movement was entirely revolutionary, women were right in directing their energies not against average humanity in general, but against their active Philistine opponents in particular. They could repulse this type of humanity, and regard it as their enemy so far as feminine problems were concerned. But the time has already come when the revolutionary has passed into the organised state, that is to say when the movement must be in normal relation to its adherents. Their demands are beginning to have results. The equity of them is being recognised, and economic conditions are rapidly preparing the way for their realisation.

Thus, both their mission and their perspective are undergoing change. That which was at first the enthusiastic dream of a few, arising from the impulses of strong and uncommon women, the avowal of natures far above the average, is now becoming the common property of the many; it is to form the new norm in accordance with which the life of this majority is to be adjusted. For it stands to reason that among these there are more average than independent spirits; persons who cannot rise to the height of living their own lives in freedom undisturbed by the opinion or the conduct of the society to which they belong. They wish to understand this freedom as a new law, as a new and higher morality which every progressive person must profess.

Will the doctrines of the woman's movement justify this claim? Or is it possible that their essential characteristics are suited only to exceptional women? Must there not be a change in the average type of woman if these views are to be realised?

But why should not such a change be possible in this case, just as it has been the condition and the result of all social revolutions? Why not, indeed, inasmuch as it is contained in the very essence of development?

The demands made by the feminist movement on the social community rest on the assumption that the greater part of the female sex is capable of being raised from a state of dependence to an independent existence as soon as the pressure of outside circumstances ceases simultaneously with the pressure of the prevailing standards.

It is characteristic of periods of transition that the number of revolutionary persons should suddenly increase—probably because the pressure of prevailing standards has relaxed, and because the suggestive ferment of the new ideas has begun to spread. All those who were too weak to revolt or to assert themselves, all those who had not the moral strength to confess themselves parts of a declining type, reveal themselves at such a time, and gather together as the adherents of those who, with all the emphasis of a strong will and an unshakeable conviction, proclaim to the world that which

the weaker members can express only in faint and uncertain terms. It is for this reason that, when the ideals
of life are changed, a new type of humanity comes to
the front. Nearly every generation, in fact, has its
peculiar mental physiognomy and is more or less distinguishable from its predecessors—this is proved by
the well-known and ever-recurring complaint of the old
people about the peculiarities of youth. The progressive
element, moreover, prevails in a great many people in
their youth, although later on their minds sink back into
conservatism.

A remodelling of the average type can be effected by
a change in the method of education—that is, by means
of the influences to which any individual may be system-
atically exposed during the years of development; also
by a change of environment, that is to say, by means
of all those influences which, in the shape of external
circumstances, exert their distinct pressure. The
economic changes which are so important in determining the social status of the female sex are very potent
factors in changing the average type, as they render a
number of qualities useless or disadvantageous, qualities
which were formerly advantageous or indispensable to
woman, and were therefore cultivated with all the
available means of suggestion. From new duties new
capacities are evolving. Did not the Englishman Bury
regard the possibility that women would develop new
characteristics as the strongest argument in favour of
woman suffrage? "Such a possibility," he wrote,
" has not arisen for nearly two thousand years."

It is true, indeed, that if " woman " in the future
must be independent, self-sufficient, strong-willed,
energetic and the like, the tyranny of the norm will

again be brought to bear, with all the self-deception and hypocrisy in its train which generally arise when superficial standards prevail.

But the demands of the feminist movement do not imply such a levelling-up, even supposing that the raising of the average were too optimistic an assumption. Its very nature as an effort towards freedom, the idea of free, individual self-government which is its starting-point, its basis and its distinctive sign, will always make it a question for the minority. In the woman's movement the female minority is fighting for a normal social status; and why should not a highly developed state of society, furnished with all the means to a heightened perception, grant, even to a minority, the position to which it is entitled?

ON MASCULINITY

THE true origin of the change which is taking place in the position of the female sex will never be rightly understood so long as the change in the conditions of life of the male sex remains unconsidered. The two sexes are in so close a relation with one another, are so dependent on one another, that the conditions which affect the one must also affect the other. One of the most important factors in the rise of the feminist movement is probably to be found in the change which is taking place in the male sex. As early as the middle of the nineteenth century a far-seeing man wrote: "The sex vices of women have now become those of men; our culture is predominatingly romantic and feminine, educating the man to be the tender mate of the woman, not the woman to be the strong, masculine companion of the man. Where mannishness cannot be eradicated, it must come to be regarded as undesirable and exceptional, and degenerate into sheer brutality; and inasmuch as men have become women, what are women to do, crowded out of their natural sphere by this sexual exodus? . . . What remains to those women who either are unable to have children or desire none, but to conquer the field which men have deserted in order to take possession of that domain which formerly belonged to them?" (Otto Ludwig, *Shakespeare-studien*).

And Goethe argues from the same standpoint when he says: "It cannot be questioned that in all civilised nations women must gain predominance. For interacting influences must render man more feminine, and this causes him to suffer a loss; for his advantage consists not in moderated, but in restricted power. If, on the other hand, woman takes something from man, she gains; for if she can increase her other advantages by sheer energy, the result is a being than whom nothing more perfect can be imagined."

The significance of these utterances lies not so much in judgments favourable to women, as in the confirmation of the fact that all is not right with masculinity. The majority of men do not realise this. It is contrary to the naïve sexual purblindness of the average man to admit that there is a difference in degree of masculinity between him and men of other periods. He clings to that measure of his masculine value which has been suggested to him from his childhood on, without asking whether this measure be consistent with the conditions and influences to which he is exposed during the whole of his life.

The conception of masculinity in modern society rules like an ancient idol which is still publicly worshipped and served with prescribed sacrifices, although it has long ceased to work miracles. The ideas connected with this are made up of remnants of bygone ages and survivals of relationships. It may, indeed, be asserted that the disparity between modern conditions of life and the prevailing standards is even greater with the male than with the female sex. By virtue of his social nature the individual man is just as dependent as the woman; in so far as he belongs to the average he is just as much in subjection to the tyranny of the norm and feels just as strongly that the decrees of customs and of morals are his lords and masters. Only the decrees themselves are different.

If we consider the conception of masculinity as it is depicted in general outlines in everyday life, or in those writings which have need of a normal basis, in pedagogic, popular medical, didactic-moral works, we find the primitive, teleological sexual type handed on from generation to generation, without having been put to the test of the actual conditions of life. In this, masculinity equals activity and femininity equals passivity. Everything masculine has an aggressive bearing towards the outer world; everything feminine is defensive; man has expansive impulses and a strong will; he is enterprising, eager to conquer, warlike, and will suffer no restriction; but the female sex, by virtue of its weak will, is subject and in need of subjection, timid, peaceful, patient, etc., etc.

Even though these sex types do not apply absolutely to all so-called primitive peoples, it can nevertheless be said that the lower the mode of life the more distinct and pure are the types. Only with those peoples whose lives are lived out on a plane below civilisation is there a division of labour in accordance with this division of the sexes. There the tasks and occupations of the man perfectly express the tendencies of the primitive sexual character. This could not be more tersely expressed than in the words of the Australian Kurnai whom Ellis quotes in his book on man and woman : " A man hunts, spears, fishes, fights, and sits about; the rest is all woman's work." All the rest—namely, work in the real sense of the word—agriculture and the crafts.

The most masculine occupations are those of the savages; the most masculine man is the savage, as he is also the freest and most unrestricted. Only when a modification has taken place in the basic instincts of his sexual nature is man capable of civilisation; and in the very first stages of civilisation, when he takes over part of woman's work, man sacrifices something of the fulness of his masculinity. He becomes domestic, fettered, dependent. Civilisation and culture bring man nearer to woman; they render him effeminate; they are anti-virile. And the higher and more refined the civilisation becomes, the stronger are its anti-virile influences. As Havelock Ellis says, savage and barbaric peoples are usually warlike, that is to say, masculine in character; the industrial pursuits were originally woman's province and have a tendency to make a man womanish. Civilisation has slowly but unceasingly worked to bring about a change in masculinity by which feminine influences are gaining more and more predominance, and the warlike, and therefore, in a restricted sense, masculine tendencies, are receding more and more into the background.

There is an historical process to be perceived in this change, which necessarily accompanies the course of civilisation; and, if the primitive and original masculinity is to be regarded as the strongest—as that in which the power of the human race finds its absolute expression—a degeneration. It is easy to prove from history how often the warlike masculinity of barbaric or semi-barbaric peoples has conquered civilised peoples whose warlike instincts have been extinguished. This appears

civilisation & masculinity.

primitive vs. differentiated masculinity

to constitute an objection to the alteration in masculinity which is caused by civilisation. And so we come to the paradoxical conclusion that through civilisation— which is almost entirely the work of masculine intelligence—man himself labours to bring about the destruction of his masculinity.

But if merely the primitive side of this conception were considered, its significance would be restricted within too limited an area. In the very beginnings of civilisation another phase of masculine nature begins to make itself felt, and to divide individuals into various groups. It makes clear that two antagonistic instincts are struggling for mastery within the male sex itself. The primitive masculinity, which is based on the utmost development of physical faculties, is opposed to a differentiated masculinity which is directed to the development and the increase of the intellectual faculties —the power arising from physical superiority is opposed to the power arising from intellectual superiority.

This conflict within the male sex is not more important and far-reaching in its social consequences than the conflict between the male and the female sexes, which, presumably, is equally deep-seated. It declares itself as a continuous struggle between these two impulses for the mastery over human society. The ideals of life which they evoke operate in opposite directions, and in their final results they mutually exclude one another. Nevertheless, they continue side by side during the whole course of the development of civilisation; they assume various shapes, are transformed, blend together and manifest the strangest contradictions.

The oldest representatives of these ideals of life are the warriors and the priests. In them the conflict between the masculine impulses is most clearly visible. Again, the struggle for predominance is shown by the status attained by these types in the earliest social communities. Whilst with barbaric peoples the warrior occupies the highest social standing, the priest in even the most ancient civilisations has been ranked higher than the warrior. In the guise of the priesthood the differentiated masculinity first triumphed over the primitive. It is true that the ideal of a rank or a caste was not always realised in the individual; in the priesthood itself the antagonism between the external conditions of life and the bent of the individual has often led to degeneration of the worst kind.

Theoretically, the Christian epoch represents to western civilisation the predominance of priestly ideals. But in practice warlike masculinity has never—not even at the period when Christian thought possessed the strongest suggestive power—been absent when circumstances required it. During the whole of the Middle Ages the antagonism between these heterogeneous ideals is easily discernible, and if the men of the early Middle Ages set aside reading and writing as an occupation for priests and women, from the standpoint of warlike masculinity, they had every justification for doing so. They suspected rightly the traps in which the elementary impulses of masculinity were to be caught and broken, the temptation of a mode of life which was to annul the distinction between man and woman.

The relations between the priestly and the feminine ideals have always had a somewhat degraded aspect in the eyes of warlike masculinity. To them, peaceful, contemplative persons are not wholly men. Those, on the other hand, who, because the deepest need of their natures demanded that they should be spared all conflict and violence, have created for themselves a heaven in which life, in the shape of the most sublime spirituality, is imagined as an eternal, ecstatic vision, regard the warriors with a reciprocal contempt, as a lower race unfit to approach anything divine. Christian standards have carried this process of spiritualisation so far that, strictly speaking, every activity of primitive masculinity is excluded. The figure, therefore, of the pious warrior who follows his murderous calling in the expectancy of a heavenly reward is a Christian absurdity; it only shows how instincts, working subconsciously, will link themselves with theoretical points of view which have been impressed on the mind by external influences.

Something of this absurdity clings to the modern ideas of masculinity. The present time is absolutely characterised by the differentiated masculinity which has been described. It is distinguished from other periods by the development of thought and the tendency to make the means of culture as universal as possible. Its nature is technically intellectual and æsthetically contemplative. Beyond these provinces life is in a state of absolute decay—and this decadence is greatest in the province of primitive or warlike masculinity.

The struggle with the elementary forces of nature which raised primitive masculinity to such a high moral level has, by the technical mastery of these forces, been transferred almost entirely to the domain of intellectuality, where it is no longer a question of courage or physical strength, but of quickness and inventiveness. Even man's labour has been replaced by machinery. The man who tends machinery has merely a certain manual skill which in most cases may easily be acquired by women and children. It is perfectly natural that where labour by machinery is concerned, women should be supplanting men.

The ethical side of the physical superiority by which man constituted himself the lord and protector of the woman and child has also lost its significance under the postulates of modern government. The " strong hand " which in other social conditions was indispensable to the individual man and was justly the foundation of his predominance, has become altogether superfluous.

But although modern conditions are reducing the activities of primitive masculinity to a narrower circle every day, although culture itself must be regarded as the goal of differentiated masculinity—yet barbaric values will nevertheless persist in customs and in normal standards. Soldiers are still accorded the first social rank; war is still held in high honour, and everything connected with it is surrounded by a halo of supreme importance and distinction.

II

WHEN Friedrich Nietzsche endeavoured to give to the future generations a canonical book of new life values, he made Zarathustra say: "Man is made for war and woman for the diversion of the warrior." He wanted to reinstate the primitive instincts of man; in the old antagonism between warrior and priest he took the part of the warrior, and to the priest he ascribed the blame for the poisoning of life.

But even supposing this dictum of Zarathustra's were suited to the natures of the majority, a warning to the coarse, the vulgar, the materialistic to avoid sinking into stagnation, or were it even to indicate to the exceptional how they might escape the evils of effemination, is there a possibility of again cultivating primitive masculinity under modern conditions of life and of preventing its decline?

Three phases may be distinguished in the course of this decline. The first goes back to the period when agriculture and industry passed out of the hands of woman into those of man; here the unwarlike individual is given a social function and value; he who, until then, had been useless and despised. In this lies the foundation upon which are reared the antitheses to the instincts of masculinity. The second phase can be reckoned, so far as European civilisation is concerned, from the time when the use of gunpowder, in warfare as well as in the chase, gave to those two distinctive expressions of primitive masculinity an entirely different character. The third phase, the one in which the ruin of primitive masculinity becomes glaringly apparent, is brought about by the predominance of machinery, and begins about the time when the civilian laid aside the sword—a visible sign that he had handed over to the State the chief right of warlike masculinity, the right of self-defence.

To the great credit of the Asiatic people be it said, that within the circle of their own civilisation they made use of the discovery of gunpowder chiefly for æsthetic purposes, and delighted in dissipating its deadly powers in the shape of elaborate fireworks. Were the men of Europe so much more brave and warlike when they created with this material the most terrible and murderous of all weapons? Or was it merely because the stronger instincts of primitive masculinity had already left them?

No man possessed of really warlike feelings would ever have adopted this weapon. The warlike element in masculine nature has its origin in neuro-muscular activity. In general the male sex is brave and aggressive on account of its muscular strength, while the female sex is timid and passive because of its muscular weakness. All these proofs of exaggerated vitality which impel man to express himself in battle arise from the consciousness of his physical strength. War is the state in which primitive man is essentially in his element, that is why most barbaric races look upon war as the normal life of a man.

Warfare really consists of outbreaks of aggressive impulses, and the weapons with which it is carried on are suited to the needs of those who wield them. They make possible an individual bravery which determines the degree of manly worth, and they afford protection to the warriors either through personal dexterity or by means of external safeguards such as the use of the shield and a coat of mail to protect the most vital parts of the body. The sword, the rapier, the lance, the spear, even the bow and crossbow, are manly weapons.

This cannot be said of firearms. Firearms are cowardly; through their use an attack becomes merely a murderous ambuscade and defence a passive and fatalistic acceptance of the inevitable. The courage which drove the man armed with shield and sword into battle was a natural expression of manliness; but that which the modern man thinks he displays when baring his breast to the pistol of an antagonist is not courage in the real sense of the word, but the sickly decadent product of a Christian ascetic self-conquest and of an atavistic masculine bravado. It is not without signific-

ance that in his *Manuel Venegas*, in which he seeks
to portray a type of proud, high-minded, self-mastering
manhood, Pedro de Alarcon, the Spanish poet, makes his
hero disdain firearms as treacherous and cowardly, even
in a fight with a bear.

What evil has been brought into the world by these
cowardly and treacherous weapons since the refinements
of modern science have brought them to a state of
horrible perfection! The immense change that has taken
place in warfare by reason of technical improvements in
firearms in conjunction with universal military service
is without a parallel in history. The wars in which
mercenaries were engaged and which provided a career
for all those intractable, adventurous young men who
were temperamentally averse from peaceful industries,
were never—whatever evils they may have induced—
anything more than expressions of elemental masculinity,
to be suffered like any other inevitable phenomenon
inherent in the nature of things. But the mad, Moloch-
like spirit of massacre which informs present-day warfare has no longer anything in common with the instincts
of masculinity. Can there be any question of individual
bravery in face of these terrible engines of murder, these
explosive shells which blow into fragments hundreds
of human bodies, or mow down the defenceless and
helpless hosts as with a scythe? These horrible weapons
reduce soldiers to mere living lumps of flesh and blood,
permitting themselves to be mangled according to
orders. "From heroic days," said Richard Wagner,
"we have inherited only the slaughtering and the shedding of blood without heroism of any kind, and with
nothing but discipline to take its place." It is no
longer the highest type of active virility which finds

scope for its energies in war, but the utmost passivity, the sufferance of an overwhelming compulsion. Modern warfare has lost its manliness and has become stamped with effeminacy.

One has only to read any truthful description of war as it is seen by the ordinary soldier in the ranks—one of those rare descriptions which are not coloured by sentimental ideas of military glory—in order to realise that no trace remains of the traditional feelings which formerly made warfare a school for manliness. Emile Zola has brought this home to us in his *Débâcle*; and we have convincing evidence in the words of a Prussian soldier who took part in the Spicheren engagement of the 6th of August, 1870: "Heart-breaking misery, despair, fear, terror, ill-disguised shame—all these things were to be seen in the faces of these poor wretches doomed to die, but no longer any trace of glowing ardour, nor any fanatical lust to slaughter or to be slaughtered. . . . Like so many chickens, when a bird of prey has swooped down and carried off one of the flock, we huddled instinctively together, trembling, our nerves shattered, each of us crouching behind the others for shelter. . . . Pale as death, breathing hard, our hearts palpitating, our limbs quivering, there we remained awaiting pitiably the Dread Thing that was coming. In truth, the instinct of self-preservation is often stronger than all good resolutions, and a mere movement would have been enough just then to have broken down the bonds of discipline. Then, a certain restlessness in the battalion having betrayed the critical condition we were in, I saw our Commander galloping towards us, and heard him shout in sharp, clear tones audible above the thunder of the

cannon : ' Officers, make ready—draw revolvers ! ' "
(*More Light in Our World*, Gustav Müller).

Thus are our modern warriors driven into battle
between two fires : in front of them the rifle-muzzles
of the enemy, behind them the revolvers of their superior
officers ! In the case of quite rough, uneducated soldiers,
the sight of blood is apt to evoke a blind Berserker
fury, in which they recklessly fire away their ammuni-
tion. What is most terrible, however, is the plight of
those who must fulfil the same duties as the professional
soldier although divorced by all the influences of
civilisation from the instinct of the fighter, and accustomed to the sheltered existence proper to their intellectual calling. Universal military service is a Tower
of Babel in its confusion of the instincts. What
qualifications for military service are to be found in an
artist, a scholar, a teacher, or an official? In all
previous epochs of civilisation, war was the affair of a
certain distinct class, and all those who were occupied
in peaceful affairs were exempt from it, unless they
themselves volunteered their services. But general
military service, as it exists on the continent of Europe,
is the worst form of slavery with which a free humanity
has ever been burdened. Through it, all men become
the bondmen of their State; they must at regular in-
tervals give up freedom as citizens in order to submit
themselves to the discipline and prejudices of a class in
whose privileges as a rule they have no share. And as
they are forced to adopt in their private life the conception of military honour, which is entirely based upon
the primitive masculine instincts, they are decidedly at
a disadvantage when compared with professional
soldiers. If the primitive instincts were stronger in

these civilians, the regulation forbidding them to carry
arms in spite of their military service would be intoler-
able to them, as would be also the idea of being obliged,
unarmed, to associate with their armed fellow-men.

If, therefore, the military profession in our modern
state of society is accorded all the honours which,
according to primitive ideas, were due to the warrior as
the finest type of manhood, this can only be described
as atavism. For war is so rare an occurence that not
every generation of recruits has any experience of it;
and it cannot be held that such distinctions are warranted
by the activities of the military in times of peace.

The deterioration in the primitive masculine instincts is not less marked in modern sport than in
modern war. When compared with the dangers which
were run by men of earlier times in pursuit of game—
dangers which, in conjunction with the quarry, constituted the real value of the hunt—a modern "drive" is
something ridiculous and pitiful. If any fatigue or
danger be involved at all, it is for the drivers, not for the
sportsmen. For any man of natural instincts it would
have seemed a repellent, and even contemptible, thing
to stand in safety shooting down great masses of harmless, defenceless creatures, driven deliberately past him.
The satisfaction afforded by his own marksmanship
could not have blinded anyone, whose instincts were
not already in this respect perverted, to the unmanliness
of such a proceeding. And yet this kind of "sport"
is regarded as a fine masculine avocation, just as though
it were comparable with the bold and courageous hunting of bears and wolves and other wild and dangerous
beasts!

The masculine instincts do not show up much better

even in those other forms of sport in which such violent exertions of the body and feats of endurance are involved as may entitle them to be reckoned as accessories to primitive virility. Accessories they are, of course, in so far as they entail the development of the muscles and of will-power, but they cannot be reckoned as achievements. Sport remains merely a game; that is why even the greatest sporting records—though there may be much to say in their favour—can never attain a heroic character such as appertains to courage shown in the face of real danger. A mere parade of the masculinity arising from bravado is all they can produce.

But if we wish to see the most perverted and ludicrous caricature of the primitive masculine instincts, we must turn to the Duelling-Code of our German students. For here we find something in the nature of an atavistic manifestation in a class of individuals who are destined to be representatives of the modified or differentiated form of manliness. This error might be disregarded as a piece of juvenile folly if it found its expression only in the actual duelling encounters, with their not very serious blood-lettings which testify so absurdly to the " untamed nature of man "; but as these encounters are accompanied by the obligatory consumption of alcohol, with its frequently degrading results, the whole institution in its present form presents one of the worst symptoms of the decay of masculinity.

Decay, constant and unavoidable decay! Do the careers that are pursued by our men of intellect still retain anything in common with the instincts which characterised masculinity in its primitive form? The Government office, the court of justice, the counting-house, the studio—they are all but sepulchres of essential mas-

"Neurasthenia" : (handwritten marginal note)

culinity. The great cities are its veritable cemeteries. Here all those dangers that brought it into being are eliminated. All the influences of life in great cities tend to produce the very infirmity which has least in common with masculinity—nervous disease.

All this shows how liable to modification are the characteristics which we are inclined to label once and for all as masculine or feminine. It is the habit to regard the nervous system of men as more resistant than that of women, and to consider as one of the important differences between the sexes the greater sensitiveness which is attributed to women, and which involves them in a tendency to react more rashly and with less restraint to influences from without. What is generally thought of as "the masculine sense," though it is far from being found exclusively in men, consists in self-control and undisturbed presence of mind in the face of external influences and impressions, and depends primarily upon the resistance of the nervous system. But the weakening of the nervous system which is brought about by the life of the great cities is also intensifying the nervous irritability of men and modifying the traditional idea of the sex.

Neurasthenia, the typical disease of the great city, is the deadliest enemy of primitive masculinity. One has but to think of the psychical manifestations which accompany neurasthenia—the depression and moodiness, the unreasonable fear, nervousness and indecision, all symptoms of hyper-sensibility to realise that the sufferer from this malady has all the characteristics of a womanly, or, one might rather say, of a womanish type.

To men of the intellectual callings the effects of city

"the masculine sense" (handwritten marginal note)

life are less injurious than to others, for the conditions under which they follow their careers are not incompatible with the less serious forms of neurasthenia. These conditions involve in many ways a considerable diminution of the aggressive instincts, and the full force of masculine impetuosity would be more of a disadvantage than an advantage to them.

Therefore, the life of the great cities does not necessarily tend to the deterioration of the masculine sex; it is in conflict merely with the primitive ideal of masculinity. To accept this ideal would be to close one's eyes to the entire evolutionary process of civilisation. It cannot be reconciled with the spirit of progressiveness. Heroism in battling with physical dangers, which brought out all that was noblest in primitive masculinity, has for the greater part lost its field of action; the tasks that are still available for its operation grow steadily fewer, for life is now governed by new aims which call forth those who possess the necessary qualities for their fulfilment.

The darker sides of this primitive ideal of manhood have always obscured its advantages. It has made of man the most wicked beast of prey among all the creatures of the earth; it has turned all life into a battle-ground; it has sanctioned murder and made the shedding of blood a joy. Only when the consequences of its gradual disappearance have become impressed upon the social consciousness may a new day for humanity be said to have dawned.

III

AND thus would come about the possibility of attaining an infinitely higher form of manhood than has been presented by any previous epoch of civilisation. The circumstances responsible for the disappearance of the primitive male instincts would place this higher type of man at the head of civilisation, in the rank due to him as its creator.

But when one regards this higher or modified type of manhood, or, to put the matter in concrete form, surveys men of intellectual callings in the light of prevailing conditions and opinions, one meets with disillusion. In almost all other civilised times and countries the qualifications fitting a man for an intellectual life have been appraised more highly by social traditions than in the Europe of to-day. In this respect European civilisation, although it may possibly have removed masculine life further from its primitive forms than ever before, is far behind the civilisation of ancient times or of the East. Whether he who stands highest in the eyes of the general public be the man of letters, as in China, or the ascetic, as in India, or the priest, as in Egypt, it is always the higher type of man, the man who is notable for the highest spiritual attainments, to whom the first place is allotted. Even the Middle Ages gave precedence to the priests, however seldom the individual priest might have realised in his character the qualities to which this precedence was due.

We look in vain for any such standard of appraisement in the social traditions of modern European civilisation. It is no longer in the sphere of priestly ideals of life that masculine civilisation establishes its creative power, for the chasm that gapes between modern thought and traditional religion has deposed the priest as the exponent of spirituality. His very existence is dependent upon an outlined interpretation of the world which excludes him from participating in the living process of intellectual development; and the halo surrounding him as the intermediary between the Kingdom of God and our ordinary earthly existence has faded away like the Kingdom of God itself. He, nevertheless, still enjoys a pronounced ascendancy of position over those whose intellectual labours have destroyed the ancient interpretation of the world: for his vantage point is based upon the conscious, ethical recognition of a higher type of humanity, incarnate in the priest, and in the antithesis to primitive masculinity which is offered by his well formulated ideals of life. This is quite compatible with the fact that in a time like the present, so replete with the products of decadence, external considerations of power may produce a paradoxical community of interests between the army and the church.

The men of spiritual temperament who belong to no church lack the consciousness of this antithesis; consequently they are unable to create out of their aims in life a new order of manhood endowed with a normative power.

Great as may be the weight of masculine thought in that form which it assumes in modern science, even so scanty is its practical moral value among the forces of modern life. The modern man suffers through his intellectuality as from an illness. Either it degenerates into intellectual extravagance, as in the case of the scholar, in whom this side of his nature develops out of all relation to the totality of life; or else it has a disintegrating and unbalancing effect upon him, as is so often the case with the average man of culture. He is neither one thing nor the other, neither a fully developed man of thought nor a primitive man of action. He is forever wavering between the two spheres, impelled hither or thither first by choice and then by necessity. His struggles towards refinement and improvement, towards existence upon a higher plane of thought, result only in producing a state of incurable discord within himself.

Is it not amazing that men whose intellectual development has qualified them for taking a critical view of everything should remain uncritical in regard to the conception of manliness? They accept the evil results that come from the incompatibility between the accepted idea and the actual condition of things, rather than expose themselves to the suspicion of unmanliness. To achieve manliness, sheer unadulterated manliness, is their ambition, and they are all oblivious to the brutal or the base or the corrupt in any transaction, provided that this tallies with the traditional concept of manliness. This fear of appearing unmanly, of displaying any lack of that virility attributed to the primitive ideal of the sex, serves to maintain all the preposterous atavistic prejudices, all the senseless, incompatible tendencies of which the life of the modern man is so full.

How vacillating and uncertain, however, are the ideas which underlie this sense of honour concerning manliness! Let us examine the idea that the more manly a thing is, the nobler it must be in a case in which it is not concerned with woman; for instance, in the matter of national self-esteem.   It is well known that the Latin races consider themselves manlier than the Teutonic. Mantegazza, for instance, speaks of the more womanly methods of love of the "blond German."   The Germans, on the other hand, ascribe womanly characteristics to the Slavs—a piece of national assumption expressed by Bismarck in his speech to the Styrian Deputation in April, 1895.   "I believe," he said, "that we Germans, by God's grace, are fundamentally stronger; I mean, manlier in our character.   God has established this dualism, this juxtaposition of manliness and womanliness, in every aspect of creation, and therefore into the European constellation as elsewhere. . . . It is not my wish to offend the Slavs, but they have many of the feminine advantages—they have grace and cleverness, subtlety and adroitness "; and on these grounds he counselled the Germans in Austria to bear in mind in all their relations with the Slavs that they, the Germans, were the superior race and must predominate, "just as in marriage the man ought to predominate."

Those, however, who are familiar with the literature of the Slavs know what a less flattering picture they paint of the German man; in their eyes his national idiosyncrasy is not superior manliness, but a coldly calculating, avaricious, arrogant, thick-skinned nature. And, in truth, appraised by the standard of more refined forms of manhood, and sensibilities developed beyond murky sexual prejudices, a standard such as appears in Gontscharow's *Downfall*, in Dostoieffsky's *Idiot*, in Tschernischeffsky's *Tales of a New Humanity*, the Germans have little reason to consider themselves superior.

If we look for a definite formula for the ideas which, in contrast with the primitive masculine instincts, are bound up with the higher order of manhood, we may find it in a transition from the physical and the materialistic into the spiritual. In this particular war, as man's most distinctive calling, seems, metaphorically speaking, to admit of such a theory. War with material weapons has given place to war with spiritual weapons; the battlefield is to be found in the realm of thought. The masculine element remains the contentious one even in the world of intellect.

This, to be sure, is only a generalisation. At all periods women have taken part in these spiritual struggles in so far as the customs of the period have allowed; and the figures of notable women are as conspicuous in the annals of religious movements as in those of social revolutions. On the other hand, an existence free from strife has always been desirable for certain intellectual types of men, for the artist as for the scholar; and only a blatant, ignoble age, in which everyone who would count for anything must espouse some faction, would be so regardless of the value of the contemplative temperament from which blossom the noblest flowers of the mind, as to force the artist and the savant to assume a warlike part.

With regard to the field of politics, which bears most resemblance to the traditional idea of warfare, and which has been held to lie chiefly within the sphere of masculine activities, we may cite Burdach to the effect that women are really better equipped for politics than are men; while Havelock Ellis remarks that the game of politics certainly appears to develop specifically feminine qualities in those who are occupied by it.

This by no means involves a compliment to women if we bear in mind the tendency of the modern systems of election, which are all in favour of giving prominence to fluent gabblers, knights of the tongue, and mountebanks, who are cleverest at flattering the instincts of the crowd.

War with the pen is scarcely better calculated than war in politics to bring out specifically masculine characteristics.   Modern journalism, with its cloak of anonymity, is not exactly a school for manliness and personal courage, apart from a few exceptional phases of it; such, for instance, as the career of a war correspondent.

Perhaps we shall come nearest to understanding the essence of the newer manliness if we think of it as the power of shaping life in accordance with one's own will, as the power of controlling one's own character and career.   To lead is masculine, to be led, feminine. On the intellectual side, the specifically masculine would be found in the greater clarity of consciousness, by virtue of which the motives of one's conduct are distinctly realised, whence this realisation becomes the ruling factor in one's conduct.

In truth, all these criteria are relative, and hold good only when we are contrasting the generality of men with the generality of women.   The generality of men, when not contrasted with the type of average womanhood, would be excluded from the sphere of true manliness.   The proportion of the strong to the weak is, with men as with women, that of the few to the many.   Within the confines of the civilised world, the faculty of mastery—in regard to spiritual as well as worldly matters—is the prerogative of exceptional individuals; the great majority of men, like the great majority of women, live in a state of bondage and under the necessity of dependence.

Most men in the social community are very far from being free agents in their own lives and actions. That dread abstraction, the State, which has them in its iron grasp, from the cradle to the coffin, derives its power from their need of support. Indeed, the form which the State has taken in our own lifetime—that of a constitutional monarchy—has simply done away with the leading principle of ideal manhood, the element of initiative and the assumption of full responsibility. It is obvious that in a constitution in which the Monarch is answerable to his Ministers, the Ministers to Parliament, the Members of Parliament to their electors for every action they take, no kind of responsibility can survive; it is—at least to all appearances—not a man's personal will and judgment that prevail, but those of some authority set over him. The man must always take his stand behind the nebulous conception of the " Will of the People " in every public function.

Even the spiritual creations which the mind of man has produced and set up as objective images are so many evidences of his being ill-equipped in regard to his faculty of mastery and his fitness for responsibility. What a need of support and subjection is indicated in the belief in a transcendental God, who, whether as an angry or as a benevolent ruler, as a severe or a merciful father, governs all the affairs of men! Man, the supposed master of the world, has given himself into the hands of this God in the same way that Woman, according to his ideas, gives herself into the hands of Man.

And when he did not bow down to the idea of

Divinity he invented some other idea to which to give allegiance. Philosophy, the purest emanation from the masculine mind, has not always shown us man's faculty of mastery and fitness for responsibility at their best. The Categorical Imperative, as taught by Kant, placed the ideal man under the domination of a barren abstraction, only to end, by means of the illimitable power of causality—as Schopenhauer understood it—by becoming an absolutely impotent puppet, dangling from the cords of illusion and jerked and pulled about by the universal will in conformity with its own ends. Even Friedrich Nietzsche himself, the most uncompromising champion of man's mastery, sought to construct the mental condition of the Superman upon the feeling of dependence which goes with the recognition of the inevitability of all that happens.

Man, therefore, would have no right, generally speaking, to regard himself an an order of being fundamentally different from woman in the matter of dependence and the need of control. One might, of course, urge that there is a substantial difference between subjection to a higher abstract power and subjection to a finite human being, such as even the most strong-minded of men must be. But this would not dispose of the great mass of inferior men whose dependence, voluntary or involuntary, upon very finite human beings is beyond question.

The idea of man as lord and master is an idea which is based upon sex. Even the most parasitical of average men assumes an attitude of superiority and mastery towards woman. Strength being relative, both in regard to mind and body, it is not difficult for any man to find a weaker being by whom he may measure his superiority.

— modern men?

Thence it happens that in the eyes of the great majority the female sex is held to be the inferior, widely differentiated, as it is, from the male by its order of life and its occupation—although it would be difficult for anyone to say what there is so specifically manly in the work of a teacher, a doctor, an official, or a lawyer under modern conditions of life. The great difference between man and woman, involving the social predominance of the man, lies in the sphere of primitive masculinity. Within the sphere of modified masculinity it has no other justification than that which the sexual relationship in its narrowest sense entails.

If men in general are reluctant to admit that under modern conditions of life they no longer differ from women fundamentally, but only in externals, and if they defend their callings obstinately against the incursion of women, it must be confessed, willingly or unwillingly, that the factor in them which resists this incursion cannot really be that desire for contrast which arises in the consciousness of sexual power.

With regard to his sexual instincts, the average man lives in another world, and on a different plane of thought and feeling. Civilisation makes demands on him which are at variance with his teleological nature as a male. It is the teleology of his primitive sexual instincts that determines the intractability of the impulse which asserts itself beyond all restraint in the individual soul, and shapes the personality towards its own ends. The higher conception of manhood, on the other hand, presupposes quite another sort of relationship between the sexual impulses and the personality than prevails in the masculine subconsciousness, unqualified by any intellectual modification.

Herein, perhaps, lies hidden the chief reason why the modernised type of man does not venture to shape life in accordance with his true nature, as well as the subterranean source of that duality or discord which very few men are able to overcome, because they have never acquired any clear consciousness of it.

It is noteworthy that in proportion as the male sex progresses from its primitive conditions of life it loses the natural relationship to its own sexuality. Is it possible to imagine anything more absurd and wrongheaded than the position taken up by modern civilised peoples towards sexual matters? The hideous falsity and hypocrisy which prevail in this matter point to a serious inability in the individual to adapt himself to the conditions of social life. That the simplicity and innocence of the sexual life should in so large a degree have been lost during the relatively brief period which has elapsed between the days of classic antiquity and our own is to be accounted for only by an abnormal condition of the soul of man—supposing that this soul has been the leading and controlling factor in human society.

When masculine intellect, having developed itself in the direction of abstract study and grown out of proportion by force of " specialising " in one particular field, incurs the danger of disturbing the relation of the individual to the totality of life, then the masculine temperament disturbs its equilibrium still more by dividing the individual into a spiritual being which is lifted into the realms of a lofty intellectualism, and into an animal being, degraded to the lowest level of sexual existence. There rankles unceasingly in the man's soul the old enmity between mind and sex, the war between propagation and personality, which has placed the

civilised races of Europe in such an amazingly disin-
genuous and distorted relationship towards sexual
matters.

There are two ways in which the freedom of person-
aility may be saved from the oppression of the sexual instincts: by asceticism, the mortifying of the flesh, which
is at the same time a negation of the demands which
propagation makes upon the individual—abstinence in
this sense being merely another term for asceticism—or
by that reconciliation of the two conflicting sides of
man's nature which is brought about by love, when it
affirms propagation in the spirit of personality. For
love permits of the sexual relation being transfused with
a content of personality.

The youth of to-day progresses towards manhood by
neither of these ways. In addition to the lack of basic
religious faith which would enable him to live in sexual
abstinence until his marriage, he is also lacking in all
moral principles of suggestive force which would encourage and support him in his desire to overcome
himself. An order of society, however, which recognises
marriage as the only legitimate sexual relationship, and
which thus makes the consummation of love dependent
upon economic conditions, practically vetoes the right
to love during the very period in which Nature most
strongly urges it. This order of society, therefore, condemns the young man in the prime of his youth to
have sexual relations with the lowest order of women—
those who earn their livelihood by prostitution. It is
right that this calling should be regarded as degraded,
inasmuch as it constitutes a retrogression on the part
of women to the rudest primitive conditions; but that
the social condemnation should be limited to the woman

and should not apply also to the man who is implicated equally in this retrogression is one of those inconsistencies which are only to be accounted for by the predominance of the primitive masculine instincts and of the views resulting therefrom.

For the primitive man there is nothing degrading in promiscuous sexual relationships. Despite the large place which sex occupies in his life, it is nevertheless but loosely bound up with his inmost personality. The lack of harmony between his undeveloped eroticism and the power of an original polygamous instinct is so great that it was not necessary, nay, it was not possible, for him to bring personal emotion to every sexual encounter, and his rough-hewn nature experienced no hurt from a kind of gratification of the senses which only on a higher plane of feeling leads to a discord between the elementary demands of sex and the tendencies of a more elevated personality.

With those, however, in whom this elevation has also been perfected in the sphere of sex, this soulless promiscuity takes on a quite different aspect, for it involves a painful conflict between those external forms of life by which they are fettered and the inner necessities of the emotions.

Not without reason have the priests, those representatives of the higher order of manhood, felt the necessity from the earliest stages of civilisation of adopting a special attitude towards sexuality. Whatever strange form religious ideas may have taken on the subject, " purity," or, in other words, submission to a severer rule than that of the ordinary man, has always constituted the first regulation for the ecclesiastic. The high value attached to chastity, which seeks to base itself as a religious commandment upon man's metaphysical destiny, seems to signify that it endeavours to convert material forces into spiritual. If the higher form of manhood consists in the development and intensification of the power of the mind, that is, of an intellectual ascendency, it must, above all things, differ in this from the ordinary, sensual form of manhood; for in overcoming instincts which have had the effect of enslaving the personality, lies the source and means of all spiritualisation. The sexual instinct is the most dangerous enemy to self-mastery in a man. In seducing the individual into sinking below the level of his personality, it assumes the aspect of an irresistible force and destroys the consciousness of that inner liberty which springs out of the ability of the higher impulses of the will to resist the lower.

In an order of society which offers man a choice between an inconceivable and impossible continence or a degrading indulgence, the noblest and most sensitive individual, so long as his financial standing does not permit of his marrying, must fare the worst. Sex assumes a mystic nucleus in the soul of the man of refinement —upon this point we need not allow ourselves to be misled by the prevailing charms of attractions of masculinity. These attractions are external and superficial; they figure as mere accessories in masculine externals. But that men of intellect should be annoyed and disturbed by the presentation of this sexual problem; that they who indulge so freely among themselves in indecent jests and allusions should be afraid of nothing so much as of the serious discussion of these matters, and should prefer to close their eyes to them—this signifies that there is something corrupt in the sensibilities of manhood. Is it not the case that most fathers leave their young sons to the guidance of chance, and thus subject them to the worst physical and moral dangers, ere they finally resolve to touch upon this subject?

No words are strong enough to condemn the attitude of the middle classes towards their growing boys. Our methods of instructing girls in regard to sex may be insufficient, wrong and misguided—our treatment of boys is a crime. At the age when their organism is beginning to tremble under the shocks of approaching manhood, they are treated like sexless machines, condemned to the tedium of dull lessons and the unwholesomeness of a sedentary life—in itself calculated to stimulate perverse impulses—and are then left to make their first sexual experiences in the arms of a prostitute. They are thus in their most impressionable years allowed to blunt their sensibility in regard to this terrible degradation of love and to become deaf to the warnings of Nature. For Nature speaks as with tones of thunder against promiscuity and punishes it with the most dreadful curses—with illnesses which result in inconceivable misery for the individual and his posterity.

We need not here discuss the question whether it be really the case that "a man's nature cannot arrive at perfection without slips of conduct," as a moralist of other days comfortingly remarks; and we may leave on one side also the question whether "the same code of morality for both sexes"—the motto of a social movement—be really practicable and sound. It is not only from a standpoint of morality that the conditions in which the sexual life of almost all men develops to-day are seen to be all wrong. There are people who contend, and with reason, that marriage in many cases is scarcely on a higher level of morality than prostitution. But there is a psychological factor in this which affects the balance not a little. The consciousness of inner freedom and the realisation of personality will have a solid foundation only in those men who come off victorious over the temptations of sex in the sense of a higher determination of the will. In order that such a determination of the will may be possible, the conditions of the individual's life must be favourable. When, however, as in modern life, they serve but to expose him and the claims of his sexuality to the worst conditions, a debasement is unavoidable from the moment that personality and sexual impulse are in conflict. How could the furtive, sordid and ignoble secrecy of connection with a prostitute fail to have its effect upon the untrammelled manliness of the emotions? Its effect inevitably is to make a man either frivolous or untruthful or wretched. A blight falls upon him, and the more refined his nature the more terrible it is.

This might seem to be a woman's view and one-sided. There is no lack of men who share it, but the rigorously virtuous men are always apt to be suspected by their fellows of softness and cant. Let us therefore cite an authority—a man who cannot be accused of undue morality in his own life. Guy de Maupassant, in his story *The Bolt*, makes an old bachelor express himself as follows on the subject of sexual relationships of the venal kind: "One retains a sense of moral and physical nausea, as when one chances to handle things smeared with pitch and there is no water available with which to wash it off. However hard one rubs, one can't get rid of the stain."

In order to avoid confessing that he is stained the

man of intellect beats a retreat with his code of sexual morality to the sphere of primitive manhood, although in all other respects he has no longer anything in common with it. In capitulating to it in regard to this one point, he accepts defeat throughout the whole field. He, the representative of the highest human development, the predestined leader of the world, gives way to his own sexual impulse. Instead of being the master, he allows himself to be a victim to a social order in which primitive masculinity is triumphant, the coarsely elemental, which to sublimate and render serviceable has been the enormous task, the achievement of the thousands of years which man has devoted to civilisation.

Nay, more. He to whom Nature has been so partial, allotting to him so light a part in the work of generation compared with that of the woman, thus placing at his disposal every possibility of intellectual development, loses through his own indecision and inconsistency his superiority to the female sex. For however superior the new form of manhood may be intellectually, it cannot compare favourably with the finer womanhood in the field of ethical culture.

Moreover, whether or not sexuality bears a different ratio to the totality of a woman's nature, or whether the sexual differentiation be only the outcome of the demands on women made by men, certain it is that woman's strenuous striving after sexual purity and her exclusive self-surrender to the one man of her choice have resulted in the refining and ennobling of sexual consciousness among women. The heroism of self-mastery which women display in thus insisting upon the sexual integrity of the personality is a form of superiority which cannot but make itself felt as soon as the recognised restrictions of their social position shall have been done away with. It already places them above the newer form of manhood.

In accordance with an inherited view, this ethical superiority of women merely counterbalances the intellectual superiority of men, thus establishing a right balance between the two sexes. That, however, is a mere evasion, a cloak to conceal a pitiable state of things which men cannot control.

Perhaps the appearance of woman as a social fellow-worker may create a change in that field where the one-sided masculine civilisation has failed. We have seen that the desire to achieve this is present among women who are aware of their duties to society; whether they will obtain the necessary powers, the future will tell. The man of intellect, however, will not develop into a harmonious and powerful being until his refinement shall extend to the sexual side of his nature. To be reborn in a new masculinity, he must do away with all the prejudices and weaknesses which belong to the primitive manhood, retaining only those elements which are inseparable from his nature as a man.

WOMAN AS THE GENTLEWOMAN

FROM whatever point of view we may consider the problems that relate to woman, we are certain to encounter something hopelessly contradictory. Nowhere else do such extreme antitheses lie so closely parallel to one another. Throughout all history woman is revealed in a strange twilight, now as a superhuman, now as an infrahuman being, partly divine or partly devilish; now as a prophetess or a sibyl endowed with miraculous properties; or, again, as a witch or a sorceress obsessed by demoniacal powers. This mixture of superstition and prejudice operates in a favourable as well as an unfavourable sense. It also produces a very contradictory inequality in the social status of the female sex. It is either oppression to the point of slavery, or glorification to the point of worship. If one is to believe the psychologists, the need for subordination is something which is always a deep, inherent factor in the constitution of the feminine soul. It is a fact that woman in all ages, and among nearly all peoples, has both by custom and by decree been given into the power of man. Even in the modern state, woman, as daughter, as wife, and as mother, is condemned to a state of sexual dependence, and in her capacity as a self-supporting wage-earner, as an employé of the State, as a teacher, and as a worker, she is unmis-

takably given to feel that the female sex is considered
as the inferior and less efficient. And yet the female
sex has attained to one position in which it enjoys the
privilege of undisputed authority. Woman as the great
lady—is it too much to say that in this aspect a portion
of the female sex has achieved the most brilliant and
gratifying sovereignty? Is not the lady the true mistress and queen of the existing social order? Are not
the most valuable privileges and amenities which this
order possesses placed in her hands?

There are two things which form the necessary conditions for this existence—wealth and beauty. It is
true, of course, that descent from a so-called good family
is also an appreciable factor, but the born lady who is
not provided for by her people, or does not possess
sufficient beauty to win a rich husband and a corresponding position in life, is usually forced to descend from
her throne in order to earn her living. It is safe, therefore, to assume that beauty is the first stipulation for
the rank of a lady, and rather that beauty which is as-
sisted by artificial means, than mere natural beauty.
The arts of the toilet in which feminine taste has
achieved so great a mastery, constitute part of the most
important duties in the life of the social dame. Balzac,
not without irony, has thus described her existence:
"She loves to comb and perfume her hair, to polish
her rosy nails and cut them to an almond shape, to
bathe regularly her delicate limbs. . . . Her fingers are
fearful of touching aught that is not soft, tender, and
odorous. . . . Does she eat? That is a secret. Does
she share in the necessities of the other species? That
is a problem. . . . To garner love is the one goal of all
her endeavours, to awaken desire that of her every

attitude. Night and day she dreams of new embellish-
ments, of the means by which she may shine; and so
she consumes her life, in order to display her dresses
and wear out her fichus. She fears maternity because
it destroys her waist, but she embraces matrimony
because it promises her happiness."

During the development of European civilisation
man in all classes has evolved into a type of the utilitarian, whilst woman has become a type of the beautiful.
This is the more remarkable inasmuch as it is a subversion of the natural order of things. For among the
higher animals, as well as among savage or half-savage
races, ornamentation and the brilliant decoration of the
exterior, that is to say, the emphasising of the æsthetic
principle, is a prerogative of the male sex. The Greeks
likewise represented their supreme ideal of human perfection in the form of Kalokagathos, a man. All those
advantages which afterwards became the prerogative of
the lady—such as the exquisite care of the body, the
consummate charm of speech and attitude, the harmonious balance of physical and mental parts, the
infallible tact in the management of social forms, the
subtle measures of restraint, the considerate seemliness
of deportment—all these were considered by the Greeks
as evidences of a beautiful manliness. The crown of
creation in the time of the Hellenes was man; in the
civilisation of modern people, at least, in social life, it
is the gentlewoman.

One might, indeed, endeavour to explain this fact by
the supposition that it is due to an effective unfolding
of a specific feminine genius for affability. To be sure,
it is rather generally assumed in our day that genius is
to be found only in the male sex. But one overlooks

the fact that feminine genius usually manifests itself in
quite other fields than those belonging to man.   The
gift of expressing one's personality through the forms
of social intercourse may be considered as a distinct
feminine talent, even though it be not exclusively
feminine.

As soon as the customs of Middle Europe became
more civilised, and gave play to more refined exigen-
cies, the influence of the female sex began to exert a
decisive effect upon the prevailing conditions.   For
at that time all things in relation to the female sex
were otherwise than in ancient times, and to some
degree justified that conception of woman by means of
which she rose to a higher plane.   The patrician women
of the Middle Ages enjoyed the advantages of intellectual culture even more than the men of their class.   It
was they who, in all questions of "morality," that is
to say, of pleasing custom and irreproachable conduct,
possessed the determining word.   They were adepts in
maintaining a just proportion in all things, a virtue
which was awarded the highest honour in the Middle
Ages, due perhaps to the law which obliged the men of
that period to value most highly in their women precisely those qualities which they themselves lacked.
They were likewise versed in reading and writing,
those arts which, according to mediæval ideas, stood in
closer relation to the priesthood or womankind and
did not comport with the duties and activities of man.
It was precisely this relationship between a mode of
thought inspired by religion and the tendencies of
woman's nature, which went to increase the estimation
in which women were held in an epoch of Christian
faith.   In them the compromise between Christianity

and real life, which is expressed in Roman Catholicism, finds its first and perfect representations. Not men, but women, were the burden-bearers of ecclesiastical culture in its worldly aspects.

However high we may adjudge the significance to culture of the mediæval woman, it seems that man must be given an equal share of credit in bringing about so extraordinary a transformation. The origin of the gentlewoman may be clearly traced to the amorous fantasy of the man. The feeling of chivalry towards woman consists, by its very nature, of a modification in masculinity itself; that is to say, of a change in those ideas which are part of the erotic sex-life. One might say that in the last analysis the sexual impulse is also the determining factor in the social position of woman. A glance at the historical evolution of love-relationships will serve greatly to clarify this point.

It is sufficiently well known that love, amongst ancient peoples, was directed chiefly upon individuals of the same sex. The sexual instinct of the male dominated the Greek women in its harshest, most despotic form, and the conditions of their lives were determined by its necessities. The Hellenes and Romans of antiquity are closely related to oriental and barbaric peoples in their sexual psychology, and their erotic relations are established upon the idea of masculine sovereignty over woman's body and soul. Woman as a mere sexual being, as a chattel penned within the four walls of a dwelling over which she has no jurisdiction— woman as the bearer of children, in whose education she has no voice—such is the form which the erotics of the Greeks gave to the legitimate life of man and woman. And those females to whom men granted a greater freedom for development were excluded from all civic honours and occupied a lower place in the ranks of womanhood.

One might entitle this kind of relationship that of the primitive or authoritative. It is as primitive and as simple as the instinct of which it is an expression, and its one purpose is that of the perpetuation of the species. There is no trace of any attempt being made to unite the interests of the species with those of the personality upon a higher plane of feeling, nor of more deeply individualised relations or intellectual communion. The opposition between the rights of the species and those of personality had not yet become a problem, for the simple reason that the personality was still in embryo, or because, even in the most prominent individual women, the sexual sphere had not yet become individually modified nor permeated by a sense of personality. In this direction, too, Plato appears as the herald of a new age; Plato, that "fairest fruit of antiquity," in whose personality and ideals one may already perceive the symptoms of that universal sickness which, in the form of a separation of spirit and nature, was to determine the intellectual life of the next thousand years. Perhaps, hidden deep in the darkest abysses of the human consciousness, the final cause of this illness was nothing more than the conflict between species and personality.

In this conflict, which Kant has formulated in his metaphysics of morality, to the effect that in the act of generation man identifies himself with something which "conflicts with the rights of humanity to his own person," it was woman who suffered the greatest disadvantage. In the early Christian world, to be sure, woman, in so far as she was considered as a "sister," and not as a sexual being, was under the same obligation to conquer sex and enjoyed the same right to a non-sexual heaven as man, but she was, at the same time, considered an object of temptation for man; the creature who, in the shape of Eve, offered Adam the fateful fruit and brought transgression into the world. The less subtle minds of that time, like those of to-day, confused the object of desire with desire itself—something that is expressed very vividly in the fantastic phrase of Saint Hieronymus, who calls woman "the gate of Hell." These men, suffering from an inner discord, were able to free themselves of the painful battles which tore their souls only by renouncing woman and the duties of propagation at one and the same time. In spite of all the prominence given to women among Christian prophets and martyrs, in spite of all the well-earned evangelical pledges of equality, neither the erotic nor the legal standing of woman was in any way ameliorated in the first centuries of Christianity.

But in the development of young races the earthly element finds an æsthetic expression in the sensibilities of those who, true to their dispositions and inclinations, are closely identified with human destiny—in painters, in poets, and in the *élite* of the world which, in conjunction with poets and painters, strives to give a newer, nobler form to human existence. Life, viewed in the light of lofty and ecstatic illusions—this distinctive mark of mediæval spirituality—affects the entire sexual sphere in the shape of a cult of woman-worship, and produces a new phenomenon in the masculine soul. This modification of masculinity, which first became known when the erotic laws of chivalry made their courtly love :

appearance, is one of the greatest achievements of
mediæval times, for it created a new kind of relationship between man and woman.

The dependence upon woman to which man's
sexual nature makes him subject—a dependence from
which the men of antiquity sought to free themselves
by maintaining an absolute lordship over the woman,
in contrast to the men of ascetic Christianity, who for-
swore her entirely—this now transforms itself into a
dependence that is voluntary, honourable and joyful.
Out of the pride of noble natures who feel that they
and their kind must be their own pledge and justification, come the illumination and glorification of woman
which lie at the basis of the knightly code of sex.　If
man were dependent upon woman it would be impossible for woman to be anything but a sovereign
mistress, whom to serve would be a favour and a privilege.　The chivalry of man towards woman is bound
up with the noblest traits in human nature; with pride
which will serve only where it may also revere; with
magnanimity which turns every act of service into one
of devotion; with self-abnegation, which has joy in its
own advantages only when they are able to be of service
to others.　Every lofty feeling, every excess of emotion,
every refinement of a new civilisation, now pours itself
into the world of love and is incarnated in the living
image of the lady.　Nor is there lacking a breath of
that religious fervour which finds its expression in the
adoration of the "Queen of Heaven, that supreme
Lady, the lovely and holy Virgin, who was the veritable
God of the Middle Ages" (Taine).　Love elevates the
new generations into a state of wild and sentimental
intoxication.　Dante, who cried, "I listen when Love

speaks in me, what he reveals unto me I do indite,"
makes of his beloved a guide to the highest circles of
spirituality by investing her with a mystic and regal
cloak of allegory.   He associates her name with the
ultimate secrets of the heavenly spheres.

These chivalrous conceptions of woman have become
the basis for the life of the higher circles of European
society whose centre is established in the gentlewoman.
Even after the flower of the chivalric ideal, and the
shining forms of service to woman, had long passed
away, woman did not utterly lose the prestige of a
higher being.   But that which was once an enthusiastic
conviction assumes by degrees the form of a mere convention.   Chivalry degenerates into gallantry.

Whilst the flexible, restless, ever-changing genius of
the male sex, advancing with the progress of civilisation, masters all the means of intellectual culture, the
lady separates herself from all the living processes of
evolution and is content to be left behind in the realm
of gallantry.   To be sure, even in her now shrunken
sphere there is still plenty of room for the play of her
authority, and the history of civilisation in the seven-
teenth and eighteenth centuries, especially that of
France, is determined in many important matters by
the influence of the social dame.   But much of that
artificiality and hollowness which lay hidden behind the
external glitter of this period, and came to light only
in that stupendous collapse at the end of the eighteenth
century, may in no inconsiderable degree be traced to
all that was artificial and hollow in the lives of these
leaders of fashion.   Gallantry, that frivolous and hypo-
critical attitude, bestows upon woman the mere semblance of pre-eminence in order really to push her back

into that place among children and minors which masculine lordship is determined she should occupy. Man, doubly astute through his physical and intellectual ascendancy, makes use of gallantry as a means of protecting himself against the demands for personal power which the society lady might choose to make. In the same degree in which the contrasts between masculine and feminine culture are now vanishing, so, too, the sphere once occupied by the lady is growing narrower. From this sphere all the great and solemn problems of life are banned, the *salon* in which the lady reigns is nothing more than a modernised gynæceum, inhabited by elegant dolls whose first duty it is to ornament themselves in order that they may please.

The gentlewoman purchases her supremacy at a very dear price. In her endeavours to preserve this supremacy she is forced to intrench herself behind a reactionary tradition. As the representative of the expedient she has fallen into a very doubtful attitude towards all that is natural, for in the world of ladyhood the natural becomes the improper. She is exceedingly antagonistic towards all the innovations which would introduce a modern view of the world into the life of her sex.

In the very concept of the lady there is something that is incompatible with the concept of a free personality. Woman, considered as a gentlewoman, though apparently elevated to the supreme peak of a beautiful caste, nevertheless, considered as an individual, leads a life within very narrowly constricted limits. It is not the unhampered development of the individual, but the furtherance and preservation of a convention which shape the conditions of ladyhood. The man of the age of chivalry did not so much honour a distinct and well-marked individuality in the lady of his heart as a complex of conventional virtues and excellences. For this reason all intercourse between the lady and her knight took place at a considerable distance, and gave but little opportunity for a closer communion of lives. This element of inner alienation is inseparably bound up with the essential nature of the lady; it forms a dividing wall between the sexes, and it is impossible to push it aside without at the same time destroying something of the intrinsic quality of the lady.

It is with the French Revolution, in which the rights of personality even among women were promulgated, that the ideas of equality and communality between man and woman begin to emerge into the foreground. Knowledge of the price at which the education of the lady must be purchased, renders valueless the privileges which are bound up therein, and the urging of certain individual women towards a free self-determination creates an attitude toward men which rests upon wholly modified assumptions. They set themselves in opposition to the unworthy and circumscribed position which the law assigns to the female sex; but, at the same time, they scorn that homage of social intercourse which arises from a fantastic conception of womanhood.

Considered from this point of view the modern woman's movement is worthy of far more respect than is accorded it. For in these conceptions the movement carries with it the most valuable ingredient of a new understanding between man and woman, since it elevates into a system that which has long subsisted as a sort of undercurrent between the sexes, and fashions it into a dogma which clarifies it for the general mind, and gives it the suggestive power by means of which it may progress in accordance with its ideals.

Mary Wolstonecraft, in her *Defence of the Rights of Woman*, a book which contains all the main lines taken up by the later woman's movement, had already thrown light upon the great deficiencies which arise from the sort of education the lady must undergo. She comes to the conclusion that "it would be well if women would merely be pleasant and sensible comrades, except with relation to their lovers." This "exception," however, indicates a mere subjective limitation. Coincident with the transformation in the social standing of women, there occurs a transformation in the erotic relationship. A new ideal of love has arisen out of the type of sexual relationship which is based upon comradeship and an intellectual-physical community of individual attractiveness and self-completion.

The necessary condition for this is, to be sure, a change in the nature of man. Only those men whose psycho-sexual constitution compels them to turn for love to an individual on an equal plane, will be able to set up the idea of mutuality in the place which the idea of lordship occupied in primitive relationships, or that which the idea of voluntary subordination occupied in the chivalrous relationship. In this type of love-comradeship between man and woman one is able to recognise a survival of the antique ideas of love such as lay at the root of the sensuous-supersensual bonds of friendship between men and youths. That which Plato, in his *Symposium*, depicts as the loftiest love between a younger and an older friend is, according to modern sensibilities, nothing else than a representation of the noblest hetero-sexual relationship.

In the ideal of mutuality the woman's movement has seized upon one of the legacies which the Renaissance bequeathed to succeeding centuries. The recognition of the free personality, and the equal right of each sex to a free and unconditional development of individual traits, have already been achieved by human society in those brief and transitory periods in which culture reached its most brilliant apex.

Therefore, the so-called "complete human being," whose shadowy figure one encounters in the world of ideas created by the woman's movement, may be said to be inspired by a somewhat diluted; but, nevertheless, in the main, quite correct conception of that which was held to be a canon of culture in Renaissance times. And the fact that the woman's movement did not accept this idea in the usual course of historical evolution, but created it out of itself, can only serve to make its value to culture still more authentic.

That gulf separating the sexes which in the course of European civilisation has given birth to so many different kinds of phantoms, shining flowers of the romantic period, such as the cult of the minnesingers, and fearful and grotesque abortions of hate and madness, such as the witch-trials, now, for the first time, appears to be bridged over by the relation of intersexual comradeship. As free companions, equipped with the same expedients of civilisation, ripe for mutual understanding, and ready to explore the heights and depths of life together—in such wise do man and woman advance towards a new era to which their union will give a new significance.

Among modern women there may be found also those who believe the salvation of woman to lie in a *lesbianism? :*

complete separation from man—an ascetic, misanthropic movement, full of an arrogant over-estimation of womanhood and a short-sighted misconception of all that woman owes to the higher and finer types of manhood. Is it not possible that this aversion to everything masculine may furnish an analogue to the aversion of early Christian manhood to everything feminine —again an unsettled conflict between the species and the personality—whose battleground this time happens to be the feminine soul? Though these women, according to their beliefs and demands, no longer lead the life of the lady, they are nevertheless still rooted fast in the soil of fine-ladyism. They subject the relation between man and woman to a criticism based upon the assumption that woman is the superior being, and do not seem to observe that this is nothing more than an ingenious demand made upon the magnanimity of man. They betray something of the real attitude of the lady towards man—towards all things that refer to the secrecies of their erotic emotions—things which the gentlewoman of the old school took care to conceal with the unbreakable silence of a great worldly wisdom.

Women such as these find no charm in the idea of a relation with man based upon comradeship. But it is also true that a proportion of men—and, no doubt, the greater proportion—will by comradeship understand something quite different from those notions which they derive from their relations with women. At heart it is always the primitive masterly type which dominates the relation between man and woman. It is well-known that even in the fairest period of the days of chivalry it was only the upper classes, such as occupied advantageous positions in life enabling them to be identified with intellectual refinements, or at least with elegant fashions, that occupied themselves with this, and even within these classes the adoration of woman by no means extended to wedded life. It was not the wife, the life-companion, who enjoyed the honours of the cult, but the beloved, the remote and inaccessible wife of another.

That which, above all things, expresses itself in these three types—the dominating, the knightly, and the comrade-like—is the psycho-sexual individuality, the peculiar, inborn disposition in the attitude of the one man towards the one woman. Even though the one type or the other may emerge more pre-eminently in different epochs of human civilisation, and, according to the general circumstances, give its character to the times, they nevertheless continue to exist simultaneously side by side. The famous Greek hetairæ, the "social companions" of man, were the first to infuse the erotic relation with something of an intellectual quality by participating in the culture and interests of man. The masculine sense of dominance began to soften and refine itself in these illicit relations until finally, in the spheres of pleasant social amenities, it legalised the authority of woman in the name of the lady.

Now it seems as if the days of this authority were numbered. The concept of the lady is beginning to collapse. Something antiquated, something quixotic, is beginning to attach itself to the idea. This, however, is still most indefinite and unnoticeable, and only visible in certain lights and reflexes.

The domestic and social revolutions which cause the functions of the "house-keeping" woman to become daily more of an anachronism, are not without their effect upon the existence of the lady. In so far as a woman is forced to earn her own living, and thereby enter into competition with man, she ceases to live under those conditions which are guaranteed to her only in the sphere of social life. In business life gallantry as a form of intercourse ceases to exist. A severer law and a more vigorous responsibility reign here, and inexorably they demand other advantages than those which are suited for a woman's destiny as a lady.

The influences of a changing civilisation are perceptible also in those circles which appear to be quite untouched by modern ideas—in circles where the lady still holds undisputed sway and serves as one of the conservative supports. These influences certainly do not appear in the guise of new knowledge, nor as self-conscious demands for a free and individual mode of life—but quite simply and under different aspects—as new pleasures and pastimes in the programme of the social dame, composed as it is of pastimes and of pleasures. The first of these disguised and revolutionary elements is that of sport, which demands great physical exertions, swift and violent movements, aiming more at sureness than at grace, or perhaps only a blunting of the sensibilities which exposes itself indifferently to all manner of minor disfigurements or injuries. All this militates against the orthodox conception of the lady who is presumed to be a weak and tender creature, in need of man's protection and his veneration. That which stamps the lady as a "higher type" is the contrast she offers to the stir and bustle of mankind; for this reason all that is comrade-like in the communion of the sexes is already incompatible with the very nature of the gentlewoman. But it is precisely in the matter of sport that one cannot exclude the element of comradeship in the intercourse between the sexes. It is just here that it has won its most extensive and astonishing victories. It would be possible to apply a variation of Buckle's famous dictum with regard to the ethical mission of the locomotive by declaring that the bicycle has done more for the emancipation of woman than all the strivings of the entire woman's movement taken together.

Assuredly the concept of the lady is beginning to collapse. And the results of this process of dissolution of a historic figure will naturally soon become visible. The gentlewoman will hardly succeed in avoiding the uncomfortable stipulations by means of which she is given her privileges, and still remain in the enjoyment of those privileges.

Something very like a danger, a threatening possibility of serious losses for the female sex, begins to lift itself above the horizon. It is certainly conceivable that all the good which modern woman expects to realise from the liberty to determine her own destiny, may not outweigh those advantages which the female sex had enjoyed in the capacity of the gentlewoman. It is no less possible that the necessity for competition would tend, so far as the male element is concerned, again to ruin that refinement of instinct which manifests itself as chivalry; and, so far as the female element is concerned, to destroy once more that cult of beauty, harmony, and physical and spiritual elevation from which the gentlewoman arose.

Here we encounter a problem of civilisation. Women must overcome the old forms without resigning

the achievements contained in these; they must create
a new style of womanhood, a form of life which will
develop organically from that of the prevailing form,
in order to win room for that which the gentlewoman
never was and never could be: a free personality.

WOMEN AND TYPES OF WOMEN

I

THE judgments which men pass upon women suffer
from the disadvantage that they are based upon knowledge at second-hand and are not supported by woman's
introspective observation of herself. Women of
superior judgment possess the faculty of divining facts
directly from their own psychology; they are thus enabled
to use themselves as comparison, evidence and substan-
tiation. This subjective manner of analysis lends a
peculiar weight to their opinions. The estimates of
" woman " as reflected in the minds of women such as
these, must at all events prove an important contribution
to feminine psychology. This, to be sure, would possess
only a theoretical value. A practical value, such as
might serve for a line of conduct or a canon of education, these opinions by no means possess, especially since
the feminine champions of specific womanhood have
not yet reached any decision as to just what is to be
understood by this term.

Let us take the case of two prominent and keen
observers, Lou Andreas-Salomé and Laura Marholm.
An attempt made to compare the opinions of these two
women relative to this point will immediately bring us
to positions in which the most opposite peculiarities are

considered as forming the basic nature of woman, although both writers establish their conception of feminine psychology upon physiological hypotheses, and therefore upon what appear to be the most reliable and unmistakable fundamentals.

Whereas Laura Marholm adopts a very generally-accepted idea and depicts woman as a being uncentred in herself, without significance, and unable to exist alone, Lou Andreas-Salomé considers her as a creature complete and integral in herself, in whose original and essential being there is to be found both self-sufficiency and self-justification, a being which, when compared to the male, appears " like a part of some archaic and lofty aristocracy established in its own castle and estate." Woman, according to the Marholm definition, does not find her centre of gravity in herself, but depends on man for her entire spiritual existence: " the significance of woman is man." Moreover, in addition to significance, man also gives her form. " All that woman happens to read about herself serves as an example and a guide for her to become as man conceives her. It is the nature of woman to mould herself according to some form and to ask for a form according to which she may mould herself."

On the contrary, the Saloméan woman is likewise representative of a very widely-accepted opinion. She is one " who endeavours to realise with every possible means of development an ever broader, ever richer unfolding of her innate self "; she feels " that satiety of the creative repetition of oneself, of the concentration of all forces within the field of self-production so characteristic of everything feminine." She creates a world for herself conformable to the peculiarity of the female egg-cell, which encloses itself in a circle beyond which it does not attempt to penetrate. Therefore, even by so elemental and primitive an indication as this, the feminine nature is shown as partaking of a fuller harmony, a more complete rounding out—an inherent preliminary consummation and entirety."

Laura Marholm's woman is characterised by the dependence and lack of self-reliance which always accompany the act of receiving from without : " she is unable, therefore, to break with convention, for this is her only support." And the convention is not only without, but also within her. " It constitutes at once her most intimate feminine modesty and a guide-line for her feelings." But the woman of Frau Andreas-Salomé " is swayed, far more deeply than man, by a hidden contempt for what is traditionally accepted. It is not the most womanly woman who feels the greatest need of a home, of morality, and of a sharply-defined sphere in order to realise herself as a woman; it is rather an evidence of her creative power that she is able to build up all this out of herself. Paradoxical as it may sound, one may nevertheless declare that the home, morality, and their restrictions exist chiefly for the sake of the man." It is only because so many external necessities rule over woman that the opposite appears to be true. Lou Andreas-Salomé very emphatically utters a warning against the common misconception which would regard the two sexes as mere halves—" as is the case with that popular idea which considers the feminine as the passively-receptive vessel and the masculine as that of an actively-creative contents."

" The human being as woman " is, according to the Saloméan concept, a composite of all those peculiarities which may be adduced from the physiological demands

of the female organism and a modernised analysis of
what has always been considered specifically feminine.
Hence, likewise, the opinion of this writer that all those
old existing designations of woman's nature—" Domes-
ticity, Religion, Modesty, Subjection, Chastity, Neat-
ness, and so on," are in no way mere incidental terms,
but, no matter how roughly or loosely regarded, symbols
and illustrations of the true nature of woman and her
attributes. According to Lou Andreas-Salomé, this
disposition permits of no complete individualisation;
woman has always more of the quality of the purely
sexual about her than has man. For it is remarkable
that woman always has a closer resemblance to woman
than man to man. Thus the saying, " one woman is as
good as any other," which shameless and brutal sen-
suality has used with regard to the woman forcibly
possessed, may become true in some noble and
mysterious sense. Woman is the less individualised
because she still has " a direct share in the universal
life itself and the power to express herself as though she
had become its personified mouthpiece." It is for this
reason that woman in her exclusive world possesses as
a constant quality of soul that which man, restless, lost,
and speculating upon the infinite, never attains save in
his rarest moments.

The method of Lou Andreas-Salomé, which explains
the conventional in order to find in it points of
support for an outlined picture of a universal type of
womanhood, precludes the delineation of the individual
to such an extent that it even refuses to recognise it as
an attribute of woman's nature. This principle is at
the same time the premiss by which this method of
generalisation justifies itself.

According to the point of view held by Laura Marholm, this method of generalisation leads in itself *ad absurdum* simply because her " woman " is distinguished by a more individual stamp and, instead of a mere creature constructed according to a scheme of species, asserts herself as a real, essential being.   What contradictions are united in this woman, out of what strangely incompatible parts is she composed!   Before all there is the " central point " or focus of woman, " that burning fountain . . . which contains woman's all, her goal, her genius and her significance, her spiritualised and inherent sexuality."   Therefore, it is not for man " that the act of selection is of chief importance, but for woman."   To be able to make this selection with an unerring delicacy of feeling— " as in a waking dream to choose out of thousands of indifferent or repugnant men the one organically-sympathetic lover "—that is considered by this writer as a faculty of the highest, most cultivated type of woman.

But it is with astonishment that we come across the passage, " It is not so much a matter of importance *whom* woman loves as that she *should* love."   We are told that the more honest, warm-hearted and worthy the man may be, in that same degree does he demand a great love in which he may display his full earnestness —whereas woman prefers that " little love " with which one plays!

The most remarkable state of affairs, however, seems to be connected with the oft-discussed " wildness " of woman.   It is alleged that by means of this wildness woman is more closely linked to nature than is man.   It is therefore something which must be preserved at all costs. "The best and also the worst feminine raw material is as incapable of being led as of being bred, of being refined or civilised like man—it is composed of sheer uncontrolledness, recklessness, instinct—nothing but feminine instinct."

But in another place Laura Marholm speaks of "the limitless capability for adaptation," and the "unbounded suggestibility" of woman. She says: "Wherever woman happens to find guidance, and thus experiences confidence, she is obedient. This is true not only of the good, but also of the bad, woman," and she makes it clear to men by lecturing them as follows: "You are able to make of us anything that you choose: courtesans and amazons, reasonable beings and saints, *savants* and idiots, wives and virgins, for we yield to every pressure of your fingers, and it is part of our nature that we should follow after you!" Nevertheless, in a third book of hers, she withdraws this concession. In this book she discovers "that it is woman who forms or deforms, distorts or unfolds the life of man's sensibilities. The soul of the mother or the soul of the sister impress their ineffaceable seals upon the most impressionable sides of man's nature. So the final question in the majority of instances is not: What sort of man?—but: What sort of woman?" And finally she asserts: "It is through her children that the innermost life of woman is determined. Her most hidden treasures come to light . . . she grows into something definite, whereas she was formerly something quite indefinite."

In spite of all her strenuous endeavours to create a consistent and universally valid type of "woman," Laura Marholm nevertheless fails to give us anything but a conglomerate of separate characters which are scarcely related to each other in the most important points, not to speak of being identical.

Even the basic hypothesis of Laura Marholm contains, to be sure, a grave misconception. According to this, woman is, both spiritually and physically, "a capsule covering an emptiness which only man can fill."

But, physiologically considered, woman can by no means be described as a capsule covering an emptiness. This capsule has a most respectable contents; it produces an organism which in the lower order of animal life is so independently creative that out of its own potentiality, without the addition of any masculine element whatsoever, it is able to reproduce and perpetuate life. Laura Marholm has thus overlooked the most important fact of the feminine organism—the production of the ovum which gives to woman a morphological rank equal to that of man. One might, in passing, observe that the Marholmian man who happens to remark to his wife that he first created her from his rib, is guilty of a similar error. Even according to the Genesis of the Bible from which he borrows his illustration, it was not Adam who created Eve from his rib—but God. Even the patriarchal view of things does not equip man with any such all-embracing power as this!

Another aspect of the specifically feminine is presented by Ellen Key. Contrary to the ideas of Lou Andreas-Salomé, she endeavours to preserve for woman "an unrestricted freedom of individuality" despite the limitations imposed upon her by her physical nature. This endeavour to do justice to individual distinctions constantly runs counter to the generalising conclusions which she is forced to make in order to prove her case. In her hands femininity undergoes so many changes that at length one is at a loss to know why anything so indefinite and so purely incidental should be worthy of further discussion.

Ellen Key, to be sure, acknowledges that one single exception of feminine superiority furnishes an irrefutable argument for every woman in her demands for the fullest freedom in the control of her own destiny. And yet, in spite of this, the purpose of her investigations is nothing more than the restriction of this freedom, as may be proved by reflecting upon that which constitutes the true nature of woman. If society, as Ellen Key demands, is to place no barriers in the path of woman in order to let her prove what Nature intended to accomplish with her, would it not first of all become necessary to drop all conventional definitions of what is womanly and what unwomanly?

What purpose is served in showing the individual woman how the great mass of her sisters happen to have become what they are, or in pointing out to her a line of conduct which is adduced only from an investigation of the average?

Perhaps such presentations of the character of the sex are intended to remind us—with an eye to the antagonistic extreme positions of the woman's movement—that not all women are suited for another mode of life than that which has been their heritage. For it is quite possible that the woman's movement, by means of hasty generalisations, may here and there have been responsible for luring persons of feeble judgment into the wrong paths—and of making them ambitious of fulfilling tasks for which they were not fitted. Yet these definitions, derived from averages, tend at the same time to increase the strength of the standards which the traditions of society and the State, even without this, impose upon the individual—how greatly at the expense of personal liberty only they can know who do not happen to fit the prevailing norm.

Subscribing to the rule of experience that the domain of the spirit must be governed by the same relations as that of the body, Ellen Key seeks to find the fundamental inequality in those very things in which lie the most important functional differences in the life of the two sexes. Just as Laura Marholm holds woman to be closely identified with Nature because of her "wildness," so does Ellen Key attribute this to her motherliness and to all that lies mystically beneath the surface of reality. And "when once the power of motherliness emerges on earth in all its intrinsic glory, then shall woman, in a deeper significance than ever before, bring forth a new salvation for the world "—that is to say, when woman has once learned how to apply to a general public sphere of action that motherliness which she has hitherto devoted solely to private and personal interests.

This sphere, according to Ellen Key's own conclusions, has always belonged to man; and one is unable to realise how the historical development of a specific feminine power is suddenly to change its own course and produce an essentially different form of culture.

Supported by this criterion of motherliness, Ellen Key divides all woman, from an intellectual viewpoint, into two races: women who love, and women who cannot love. By this means she avoids being compelled to deny the efficiency of a very frequent and very characteristic type of woman, the egoistic-frigid—as is the case with Laura Marholm, who sets up a sort of intensified eroticism as the criterion of femininity.

Among those women who cannot love there are to be found "bewitching ephemeral natures, or gifted artistic souls, or great sorceresses of the senses, sometimes cold, reasonable beings, at other times, little, narrow and commonplace souls."

Whatever they may be, it is not from them that humanity need expect any addition to the feminine life-values. That may be expected only from the women who can love. "For such women the one thing that determines life is their destiny as wife or mother, sister or daughter, friend or helper." Great individual inequalities may be found even among these women. For some of them erotic love is the highest of all things, others again are more profoundly affected by maternal love, still others feel most deeply of all that universal human sympathy which signifies motherliness in the widest application of the word. But with all of them it is the power of personal surrender which gives them a distinctive racial mark. By means of this they are able to recognise one another from the North Pole to the South."

It is an old, well-known trait of the specifically feminine which lies at the root of this: the personal surrender, the capacity for sacrifice, nay more, the very need of sacrifice. In the soul-life of many women the idea of sacrifice plays a prominent part; they find a moral atonement and inner contentment in an action only when at the same time they have been given an opportunity to overcome their proper ego and its demands. They do not so much wish directly to assert their own personalities as to make room for another personality. It may indeed be true that the nature of women is really most characteristically expressed by this idiosyncrasy of theirs.

But perhaps this peculiarity is to be ascribed to nothing more than a mere product of civilisation and to the circumstance that women, standing in the dependent and servile relation of a secondary sex to that of the male, are always valued according to their dependence, or again to the fact that because of their susceptibility to suggestion they are more easily impressed by the prevalent religious laws. The ideas of sacrifice and self-denial are, as is well known, given the highest rank in the Christian religious world; they represent the noblest moral values. These ideas, to be sure, originated with men as general regulations without regard to sex—a fact which, like the entire Christian world of ideas in its symptomatic significance, is altogether too little regarded by the defenders of a specific psychology of sex. It is also to be feared that in the " universal human sympathy, which signifies motherliness in its widest application " the social and religious geniuses among men have long ago left women far behind.

Personal surrender in itself is not always, as Ellen Key seems to think, a reliable basis for the classification of those women whose racial mark it is supposed to be. Resignation to motherhood does not always signify a symptom of feminine " unselfishness." According to the entire nature of their beings, many women who are mothers belong not to the altruistic-sentimental-sacrificial type of Ellen Key, but to the egoistic-frigid. The narrow physical connection between mother and child enables them to feel the child as an appendage of their own organism, an appendage on which they lavish their love as upon themselves, because they are not as yet conscious of it as a separate and distinct being.

Instead of asserting that woman had no centre in

herself, one might with equal justice hold that she is the most self-centred of all beings and her own justification far more than man. All depends upon the type of woman that is understood by the inclusive term " woman." Who does not know to what a degree the cult of the person, the self-love, verging upon self-deification, sometimes reaches with certain women? In that type which Ellen Key describes as being incapable of loving, this element of surrender, this peculiarity which is supposed to be so inseparably bound up with female psychology, is not to be found. In spite of this —or perhaps just because of it—this type represents the mightiest and most dangerous aspect of womanhood— that of a great, wild egotism, restricted by no social instincts and equipped with all the power of a primitive force. Should one attempt to classify specific womanhood, according to the power which it exerts in life, then one is forced to give first place, not to the erotic-eccentric type—since the inward dependence of woman upon man could never signify power for her—nor to the altruistic-sentimental, which, though influenced by ideas of social reform, is only a more moderate variation of the dependent erotic type of femininity—but to the egoistic-frigid type.

These women do not usually emerge from the boundaries of the conventional, for many of the well-accredited traits of the " real woman " closely coincide with their inclinations and their needs. The drastic law of chastity is something which fits itself like a perfect form to their erotic unsusceptibility—just as that of religiosity suits their distaste for the plebeian-masculine manner of thought; the duties of the domestic hearth satisfy their feelings of self-sufficiency; the social

position of a lady gratifies their innate need for dominance and superior place.   The life led by the lady of
fashion presupposes, and in so far as it is not of man's
direct creating, is also produced by the egotistic-frigid
type.   For that reason Ellen Key's declaration that no
enrichment of the feminine life-values may be expected
from women who cannot love, does not appear to rest
upon a very sound foundation.

If the beautiful, flowery veil which the art of fiction
has cast over woman—as she is revealed by Lou Andreas-
Salomé—be lifted, then it is likely that traces of this sort
of femininity may be discovered beneath it, one and the
same original image, seen now in a warm and idealistic
illumination, now in a colder light.   This figure does
not belie its affinity with that unapproachable, unseiz-
able womanhood which shapes a world entirely for itself
—a world towards which man, a restless, careering being
without home and without estate, is for ever powerless
and for ever alien.

In this way separate feminine individualities are
capable of being arranged into groups without the necessity of referring to other sources than those of the
mutually irreconcilable statements as to " the true nature
of woman " which are given forth by women themselves.
What is most remarkable is that the women who
originate these opinions do not observe or do not wish
to observe, the differences that exist between their
various fundamental conceptions.   That 'woman and
woman may be all one, as Lou Andreas-Salomé declares,
appears simply incomprehensible, coming as it does from
the lips of a most uncommon woman.

Certainly differences so great exist among women,

that the understanding which arises from the mere community of sex is, in many cases, entirely suspended.
That searching, masonic look of which Laura Marholm
speaks, a look by means of which women among themselves are supposed to read the "secret cyphers of their
own experience," is something which is of effect only
among women of the same class—but in cases of greater
divergence, such as the differences that exist in the very
core of personality and the mystery of essential being,
it fails.

Every human being of any individuality is aware
that there exists a type to which he belongs, to which
he can make himself understood, with which he has
something in common; and also another type, the vast
inaccessible majority which, no matter how clearly he
may speak, does not understand his language, and for
which he must for ever remain a closed book. Nor
does this line of division always run parallel with sex.
In particular, women who are intellectually far advanced
usually find their affinities among men. This is not only
true with regard to intellectual instances, but in far
deeper things they find more points of contact with them
than with the members of their own sex.

II

No doubt it is in the erotic specialisation of type that
we must search for that inmost essential germ which
either separates human beings or brings them together.
All other divergences, such as those created by temperament, degree of intellectuality, direction of the will,
in short, all those innumerable variations which arise in
a single individual's elements of personality, are rooted

far less deeply than this. Not even the difference of sex is more profound.

Bourget, whose book, *The Physiology of Modern Love*, is written with the most unprejudiced powers of observation, declares that among the lies which women inflict upon men that of being sexually awakened through love is by far the most common. The incentive to this falsehood lies apparently in the fact that, consonant with certain prejudices, this sexual awakening is looked upon as a moral obligation. With man the sexual moment is allowed to manifest itself without disguise as a bare impulse which, for its transient gratification, is content with the generative act committed upon an individual of the opposite sex; but in the feminine consciousness, the sexual moment is supposed to appear only in the form of love, that is to say, it must first be aroused by a particular man. With respect to the true state of affairs, women usually deceive not only men, but also themselves. The power of moral prejudices and the forcible suppression of natural instincts which these entail is so vast in this direction that it may be doubted whether anyone, even among physicians, is able to read clearly into those inscrutable depths of the feminine soul. When Bourget speaks of women who in all things that pertain to love possess the tendencies of man, that is, women whose sex exists as "a subordinate, equally-divided life at one with the intellect and outside the heart," he touches upon a phenomenon which is considered as an "exception," not so much because of its rarity as because it departs from the norm set up by bourgeois respectability. Separate female individuals differ so considerably from one another on this score alone that it is impossible any longer to give credence to the idea that an identity of personality must perforce accompany an identity of sex.

It is, however, not necessary to confine oneself to such exceptions to woman's nature in order to meet with vital contradictions which arise precisely where the universally feminine rests, apparently, upon the most reliable basis of teleological sex character. Even the heterogeneous types of women which we have just observed are in the last analysis irreconcilably separated from one another by means of erotic idiosyncrasies.

There exists a force which, above all things, determines the personal life and historical position of woman —the feeling of dependence. There is no doubt that this bespeaks an inner need which arises from the nature of a certain type of women. And the origin of this feeling of dependence just as unmistakably takes its rise in the realm of the erotic.

Such women have need of a support, a guidance, and a law dictated to them by a superior will. Man is truly their sole significance, their head, their proprietor, and the idea of subjecting themselves to his physical and intellectual dominance sets free emotions of erotic joy. It is for this reason that they love the strong hand with power to command and forbid, threaten and compel. It is also these women who cause the man of their hearts to cling to the illusion that they are his own handiwork and creation; for they are governed to such a degree by the suggestive power of his personality that they entirely mould themselves to that pattern which best suits his taste. In them the teleological sex-nature of woman becomes most unqualifiedly apparent; their entire personality is penetrated and constantly absorbed by it.

Women of this nature form a sort of guarantee of

① erotic ~~subordination~~ submissive type)

The masochistic woman:

man's peace, if not entirely of his happiness. It is to this also that one must look for the reason why this type of the feminine is always valued so highly. Woman herself need expect but little benefit from such a type. One might rather say that something tragic is visible in her, a predestination to incalculable sorrows, to endless fears and tortures. In a great many cases the life of such women is nothing more than a sequestered reposefulness under the shelter of a wise and protecting power. But it is too often the case that by virtue of the attraction which opposites possess for each other, they fall into the hands of violent, intractable and passionate men, unto whom, because of their dependence, they surrender themselves at discretion. Who does not know such weak, patient, gentle and tender wives, who tremble before their husbands as before a cataclysm— and are defenceless against their jealousy, their suspicion, their black moods and irascibility?

It is the women of a sanguine temperament who escape most easily in this matter, those light-hearted, superficial natures, adapted to playfulness and toying, to craft and feints, those bird-and-puppet souls, mistresses of back-door and alcove tactics, who, clever and adroit, are versed in all the arts of flattery, knowing well how to take advantage of man's "weak moment." They are all sufficiently described and well known as "woman," although apart from their erotic subordination, they have little or nothing in common. Many of them are exceedingly reticent women, who seldom disclose anything concerning the secrecies and dark hidden spots of their soul-life—not even to themselves; others, again, are great prattlers who babble forth everything, shamelessly revealing both themselves and the man in whom they place their faith. Sometimes, too, it is an observable fact that the subjective illusions which arise from the erotic predisposition are stronger than the perception of real conditions. The husband is not always the stern master and arbiter his wife imagines him to be; but she loves the strong hand—and consequently he must possess it.

These women directly demand oppression, even when they must suffer under it. Just as they look upon jealousy as a proof of love—and no doubt because the jealousy of the man infuses them with a fear which gives them power to resist temptations and serves as a substitute for the lack of personal will-power—so, in like fashion, they find a certain pleasure in even more violent outbursts, inasmuch as these, being an expression of fighting manhood, serve to increase their feeling of safety. Wherever customs are primitive, as in a peasant population, even blows are regarded as a proof of the genuine affection of a man—as may be shown by the well-known anecdote of the weeping woman who, when asked the cause of her being so inconsolable, declared that her husband no longer loved her, for he had not given her a beating for an entire week.

Jacobsen, in his *Maria Grubbe*, has depicted this feeling to which primitive womankind is subject in the character of a woman who descends from the height of society into its deepest depths in order to belong to the man of her heart. One day, when he, the former servant, is giving her a thrashing, she is amazed to discover that no feeling of raging hate arises in her, and she continues to love him above all things as a man who is deterred by nothing in the world when it comes to having his will.

Moreover, the type of erotic subordination, the type

of woman which—if we are able to correlate the numerous contradictions of Laura Marholm, is presented by her—is embodied and glorified in countless figures and in literature—the best known and most characteristic being Kätchen von Heilbronn. This type may be regarded as the average, the most ordinary, the type which is usually understood when one speaks of " woman."

And yet there is evidence that this is neither the most common, nor the " normal," nor the essential type of woman.

The supposition that the emotional life of the female sex is first determined by the personality of the man is no less frequent than the assumption that woman does not seek in man a personality so much as a father for her child. Many declare that the passion of maternity so wholly fills the soul of woman that only a secondary place is left for man. For instance, to cite Krafft-Ebing : " Whereas man loves first the woman, and only in a secondary sense the mother of his children, woman places the father of her child in the foreground of her consciousness and only after that the man as husband." Or, to quote Lombroso : " The love of woman for man is at root nothing more than a secondary quality of motherhood." According to Arno Garborg : " Woman does not love as we do. Her inclinations prove that inasmuch as a father is necessary for her child, it is not so overwhelmingly important if it be this man or that man." Many others might be quoted.

In so far as the maternal women belong to the altruistic-sentimental order of their species, they have a close erotic affinity to the subordinated women, but in so far as they approximate to the egoistic-frigid type, the

Women and Types of Women 161

differences in their relations to man increase considerably
as well as those divergences which separate them from
their sisters. That woman who devotes her life to an
erotic surrender to a man can never hope to be understood in this connection by a woman whose life interests
are concentrated in motherhood. The reason why the
contradiction which prevails here is not brought more
conspicuously into the light is due only to the want of
reflection among ordinary women and to the similarity
of the conditions which are created by a common sphere
of life-interests.

Those women whose motherliness is infused with a
strain of the egoistic-frigid type do not feel themselves
dependent like the women of the erotic submissive sort:
with regard to man they have a lesser power of assimilation and greater self-reliance, because their own centre
of gravity does not coincide with his. At times, no
doubt, owing to the superior will of some man, they
are plunged into painful conflicts with their passions,
but more frequently they are enabled by means of the
will and maternal instinct to bring some man of feebler
instincts inside the yoke. They may be recognised by
the fact that they regard the children as mainly the
property of the mother, flesh of her flesh, blood of her
blood, brought forth by her with a thousand pangs and
sacrifices, and that they consider the husband to have
only a small and transitory share in them, such as was
his at their begetting. The instincts and the interests
of these women are widely separated from man's; they
feel, generally, no great desire for a really intimate community of life with him, and, despite the intimacies
of wedlock, it is only in an external sense that they share
his life.

That which gives these women such a supreme elementary power over man is the combination of individual egotism with the generative impulse; so closely do they feel themselves one with their child that this appears to give them a greater participation in the "universal life of Nature." The preponderance of their instinctive life gives rise to the appearance that woman stands closer to Nature than does man, and this exerts a powerful erotic charm upon those very men who suffer from too great a cultivation of the intellect.

With respect to "moral" rank, this type of woman is not to be given so lofty a place as masculine opinion accords her. Otherwise there would be no ground for the supposition that the female sex is so closely identified with that aspect of the generative life which manifests itself in love. The fact that love is exclusively bestowed upon a certain person for the sake of that person alone—that is the first thing which distinguishes the relation of love from a mere union for the purpose of propagation.

This peculiar characteristic of woman might even contain a certain danger for man—at least, with regard to his paternal prerogatives. It would not be impossible that as soon as the female sex obtained social power, this type of woman would force man in his position as a father decidedly into the background. Luckily for man, devotion to motherhood is usually accompanied by that passivity which is part of the primitive sex-character of woman, and precludes all independent action along the lines of a general idea.

Only the extreme type of egoistic-frigid femininity emerges beyond the boundaries of this primitive sex-character. Is not an "insatiable desire for dominion" held to be one of the ruling passions of woman's life? Is not woman, as portrayed by Lou Andreas-Salomé, a being established entirely in herself and thus quite independent of man?   Is not the prototype of Mrs. Egerton to be found in that woman to whom no man's love has ever been able to give a complete inward satisfaction—the woman who considers herself as the "flower of humanity, the crown of creation," and to whom man is only the "accidental by-product"?   To such women man in his best aspects appears as a "great comic child" at whom they laugh in their serene sense of superiority, but in his worse aspects as "an animal with primitive instincts," or even, at the very worst, as a "man-beast."   And their warning runs: "Hold thy soul fast in thy hand and do not pledge it to any man."

In this type we are able to discover something which may be compared to the feeling of lordship and superiority which is considered to be the pre-rogative of the masculine soul.   In its harshest form this kind of femininity is not very far removed from man-hating; the relationship which exists between such femininity and its corresponding masculinity reminds one of the sort of love of which Nietzsche said that "in its means it meant the war, and in its motive the mortal enmity of the sexes."

This paradox, to be sure, throws no light upon the nature of love, but only upon the nature of the sexual relationships as they are reflected in the abysses of con-sciousness.   Women, no less than men, feel that great attraction which the exercise of personal authority brings, and the most common vice of femininity, coquetry, originates in this desire for power.   Nature has given man the physical force of his sexuality, from which he

derives the consciousness of his pre-eminence. The chief
art of femininity consists in the disarming of this elemental force by means of an exquisite and sensual cultivation and the reversal of the primitive sex relationship
which exists between the conqueror and his prey. The
amorous, wanton element which is so questionable a
trait in the average woman appears as a product of the
latent war in which woman pits her sexual power against
that of man, in order to subdue the subduer.

The wanton element is a relatively harmless peculiarity
in the womankind that is erotically subservient, since
it is only an expression of a vanity which contents itself
with the desire to please, without desiring to rule: but
when coupled with an egoistic-frigid type of being, it
gives to the woman, who in addition possesses the
necessary sensual appeal, a power which is greater than
that of any other human creature.

The special and significant feature of this type of
femininity is the fact that it does not wish to establish
the superiority of woman on the sexual power of the
wanton element, but upon an independence of man
which may be able to free her from her sexual coldness,
and give her room for the unfolding of her intellect
and soul.

But the superior intellects found in the female sex
do not all come under this head. Sometimes we discover
quite another type among them—such as the women
of whom Laura Marholm declares—certainly with a
confusion of cause and effect—that they are "sick with
that inner cleavage which the woman's movement first
brought into the world." It is truly one of the weaker
aspects of the woman's movement that it endeavours to
trace the entire instinct for subordination in the feminine

soul to influences of education, and refuses to recognise its erotic basis—but the roots of the conflict in which these women suffer pierce more deeply into the constitution of the soul than does the power of theoretical opinions. That development of woman as an independent personality of which the strivings of modern women are the expression, is attended in some cases by a dyscrasy of the feminine being—a bad mixture of the tendencies of the female striving for sexual subordination and the tendencies of her personality striving for independence. Such women, by reason of their erotic peculiarity, look for these very qualities in the man of their choice which they are least able to endure in their extra-sexual life. As women they demand that which as personalities they abhor. Their sexual nature craves the lordship and dominance of the man, because their erotic emotions may be aroused only through the idea of being mastered and subservient, but their will towards self-assertion resists the tendency to subjection as soon as its consequences beyond the erotic sphere become palpable. For such there is no path that leads to a harmonious relationship on the basis of sexuality. They are doomed to unhappiness—like all other human beings in whom occurs an inner rift or discord.

The signs of this dyscrasy, as yet observed so little, despite the fact that it very often produces the fatality in ill-starred love affairs, may be traced in the destiny of many famous women, such as Mary Wollstonecraft, Marie Baschkirtzeff, and, perhaps most plainly, in the case of Sonia Kowalevska.

Attempts have been made to explain their fate on the score of the maladjustment that presumably of necessity arises out of the intellectual strivings and the natural activity of woman.   But is there not in this a misconception of the deeper causes?   Happiness in love, in so far as it is not conditioned by external circumstance, depends essentially upon an inner balance, that of an agreement between the erotic nature and the other aims and impulses of the individual life.   That love in woman's world must perforce manifest itself as a necessary feature of subordination, is an arbitrary assumption and is true only of those women who are unable to lift their erotics above the primitive teleological sex-nature.

For there exist many women to whom love by no means implies any surrender of personal liberty.   The idea of the strong hand is as abhorrent to them as it is fascinating to others—but not because they are incapable of any personal surrender.   Not the degree, but the manner of the surrender is the principal thing.   It is the custom to qualify the difference between the masculine and the feminine manner of love by asserting that woman loves with complete self-resignation and man with complete self-assertion.   This differentiation becomes totally invalid in the cases under consideration. In place of the subjective we have a .nutual relation based upon more complete expression of the being—a mutuality in which considerations of species are outweighed by purely individual ones.   The subjective ideal in which the particular erotic nature of any person is reflected assumes with women such as these the form of liberty.   The assumption so joyfully proclaimed by them is no longer that of service on the one side and of lordship on the other, but that of equality.   Natures such as these are worthy of the beautiful words of Richard Wagner, that the love of strong natures celebrates itself in the "free surrender unto him who does not choose to compel us."

Such women are easily converted into man-haters when unfavourable circumstances accidentally bring them into contact with men of a dominating kind. The current expressions with regard to man as the master of woman, and the duty of woman to subject herself and to serve, frequently bewilder and disturb them during the earliest period of youth, until they are overcome by an ascetic repugnance against all masculine love. It is only when their personalities have become independently developed beyond the prevailing standards and they grow aware that every free human being must shape his life according to the laws of his soul; or when, perchance, some fortunate encounter teaches them that individual differentiation makes quite a different being of the one man than that which they judged him to be in the mass, that they once more feel a harmony between themselves and the outer world.

It is these women who are farthest removed from the teleological sex-character of femininity. Superficial observation is prone to confound them with the type that demands prerogatives, because with them, too, the atypic parts of their nature determine the position they are to occupy in relation to the inherited order of things. Since present conditions are regulated by quite different considerations, it happens that the revolutionary and polemic element becomes more conspicuous in them than would comport strictly with the inner necessities of their being. This polemic element creates a most unpleasant impression upon those who are not participants in the cause of the "emancipated," and the animosity of the sort of man who would confer the name of

" woman " only upon the erotic, subordinate type, has branded them indiscriminately with the unpleasant term of " man-woman "—*Mannweib*. It is not to be denied that a certain relationship exists between them and the world of masculinity. Because of this relationship, which, if not judged according to a purely one-sided sexual viewpoint, may possibly be considered an advantage, one might well contrast them, as the most progressive and synthetic type of femininity, with all the others.

One point might be especially mentioned as a proof of how strikingly their sensibilities differ from those of ordinary womanhood—and that is their attitude towards the polygamous morals of the male sex. For most women the number of conquests and adventures which a man may have had are in a direct proportion to the fascination which he exercises upon them; they even regard these conquests as an advantage. The idea of the virginity of a man possesses no charm for them. Though it may not appear exactly repugnant to them, it nevertheless leaves them cold. They regard male polygamy as a matter of course and unalterable. Nevertheless, it frequently occurs that young girls, as soon as they discover these things with regard to the man they love, are plunged into a state of profound despair—although, according to the prevailing views of society, no moral blame may attach to the man. They suffer almost as deeply in their inmost sensibilities as do most men under the reverse circumstances. It is due only to the prevailing views that this conflict remains buried in the voiceless profounds of the soul, attended by those shy and silent sufferings for which there is no echo in the outer world.

It would prove no impossible task to find indications of this in the literary works of certain distinguished women. In so far as the works of an author may be regarded as documents of his personality, and the changing figures of his imagination tend to betray the nature of his relation to the world, one might, for instance, regard *Mauprat*, a novel in which masculine virginity is glorified, as an unmistakable evidence of the erotic inclination of that tender and free-spirited woman George Sand.

The fact that this feeling has found expression in certain tendencies of the woman's movement is likewise of symptomatic significance. Unfortunately, it is here amalgamated with all manner of moralising generalisations. All such moralising merely obscures the essential phenomenon, for it is not a moral judgment, but a subjective feeling—the expression of a definite constitution of soul—which has to be considered here.

The best-known representative of such a type is Svava, in Björnsen's *The Glove*, a girl who breaks with her lover when she learns of his past life. But here, too, importance is given, not to the psychological problem, but to the moralising tendency. The extreme opposite to Svava's ideas, has, very characteristically, been given to us by Laura Marholm. In her story, *What Was It?* the lover remarks to the heroine: "Love of a venal sort always seemed revolting to me. I have never yet had contact with any woman." Then, appalled, the girl turns from him: "a cold shudder seemed to go through her soul, as though she had met with some frosty disillusion."

Should one endeavour to group the types of femininity according to the analogy of primitive and differentiated types of men, it would be necessary to seek a standard in the individual erotic predisposition and not in external social differences. An established formulated antithesis to the duties of life such as exists among men is not to be found among women, and the approximate parallel of the prostitute and the honest woman would be inadmissible, because prostitution is a form of living not socially approved, the inherent disposition to which represents an atavistic defect in the individual. That which may be recognised as characteristic of primitive femininity is that inability to assert oneself which finds its expression in the feminine desire for subjection, the lack of personality which gives woman as a sexual being into the power of an alien will, whether this will take the form of parental authority in forcing her choice, or the conjugal lordship which assumes control of her person. But that woman who out of her own fulness of power desires to retain command of herself as a sexual being, and, true to an inner need, looks upon this personal right as the highest law of her life, that woman who, rather than be dependent, is content to toil—who would rather give up love than her right to choose for herself, must be regarded as a type of differentiated womanhood, regardless of the social position she may occupy. The determining feature is the development of a consciousness of personality which rises above the primitive teleological sex-character—and most comprehensively so when it also penetrates the erotic idiosyncrasy of the individual.

Moreover, one ought to guard against setting up the quality of the sexual nature as in itself a standard for the estimating of personality. In feminine matters questions of mere taste are turned into questions of principle. It is quite futile to argue which type of femininity may be the real and genuine. "What ought one to think of a woman who is content to be wholly a woman?" asked Max Stirner. "That is not possible for every woman, and many would set up for themselves an inaccessible goal. Besides, woman is feminine by nature, femininity is her peculiarity and she has no need of 'genuine' femininity." The determining factor in the life of every individual woman is the erotic attraction which she exercises and the sureness of the instinct with which she makes her choice; the universally feminine qualities have nothing to do with this. Does not an altogether private and personal standard come into force here? Is there not a law which in every case operates only according to the individual nature of the two participants? Hemmed within the confines of a distinct personality, we are unable to choose or alter that mysterious fundamental law upon which our desires and emotions are based as upon fate itself. It would be useless to attempt to come to any common understanding or conclusion where so much that is diverse and contradictory is at work in the profounds of our souls. Woman and woman are no more alike than man and man. Unless this fundamental truth is recognised, the psychology of sex will remain a labyrinth of insoluble contradictions.

FAMILY LITERATURE

NEVER before have the ordinary conceptions of femininity, of the imaginary "ideal woman," been so imbecile as in the nineteenth century. In order to understand the full extent of this stultification we must contemplate the picture of femininity which is afforded by that literature which is written especially for women. For the present age has this questionable distinction—it possesses a special literature for women.

In the various epochs of ancient civilisation previous to the decline of Rome, there was no feminine "literary public" whatever; women were not admitted to the theatre, and their lack of education, their inability to read, as well as their circumscribed life within the house, prevented them from having any access to poetical productions, whether written or recited. Yet ancient literature presents us with a richly individualised picture of woman, especially in the form of feminine deities.

On the other hand, in the Middle Ages it was precisely the women who, together with the clergy, were the supporters of culture. As arbiters of refined manners and of fine and genial social life, they far excelled the priesthood. Women were also the chief patrons of secular poetry, nor did this exert any cramping influence either on its subjects or on its modes of expression, though written especially for them. In this literature, too, woman greets us in a rich array of personalities, many of them, such as Kriemhilde or Isolde, or the women of the Charlemagne epic, being far removed from "the pattern of ideal womanhood" which we are now accustomed to admire.

This "pattern," and the literary precautions which are taken to protect it, are creations peculiar to the present age. Goethe, to be sure, complained to Eckermann of the effect on dramatic art of the presence of young girls in the theatre, but since then this influence has increased enormously.

For now there are two distinct provinces of literature. One is the province of free and personal creation wherein the individuality of the author, his own experience of the world and of life, reign supreme. But in this province the greater part of the output of our printing presses from year to year finds no place. Circulations by the hundred thousand, which bring so much work and so much profit to authors, and are such a feature of modern literature, are the emoluments of a far different field—that of so-called family literature.

Everyone is aware that the phrase "family literature" is not an honorary title. It is not the literary quality of the work that is regarded, for artistic excellence is not the point of view of its critics. No honesty of observation, no creative power, invention, nor new problems which denote literary development are expected here. Whether the works be literary or scientific, novels or poems, treatises or anecdotes, they must all be made according to a fixed pattern, must have a certain sort of moral foundation, and a certain conventional relation to reality, or they will never pass the censorship of the family journal. This procedure is, of course, most fatal for the purely literary production, since the chief object of the system is to provide mental food for the family table. The world which must be here represented has to be enclosed within a sort of Chinese wall, and the characters must play their parts according to fixed rules. It is a puppet show in which a number of stereotyped figures and thoughts perform with constantly repeated variations a fable which is conventionally supposed to represent the ways and works of human beings.

Arthur Zapp, in a very significant article which appeared in the *Zukunft* of the 12th of November, 1898, has, frankly and without reserve, shed some light on the terrorism exercised in this field. He describes the thorny path along which he was driven from being an independent creator, working according to his own impulses and observations, to becoming a manufacturer of novels for the family circle. He quotes some very instructive passages from letters which were sent to him by editors of widely-read family journals. One of them writes: "We cannot accept contributions that have a political or religious character. In the matter of love and passion they must contain nothing which would prevent them from being read to the younger members of a family. Cases of divorce or suicide must not be introduced. The story must be increasingly interesting, and in each chapter some fresh event must occur or some new complication must arise. The ending must be a happy one, leaving a pleasant impression." The editor of a journal which has a circulation of over a hundred thousand, writes in a marvellously similar strain: "Our publication is intended for the family circle, so we must, above all things, lay the greatest stress on decency and an absolute avoidance of all political and theological controversies. The stories must be terse and full of incident, maintaining the reader's interest and avoiding wearisome descriptions and reflections. A satisfactory termination is indispensable." Whenever the author permits himself to be tempted away from conforming to this pattern of "family-journal-novel-manufacturing," as he himself calls it, whenever he describes an environment or dissects a character psychologically, or even attempts a satirical attack on the weaknesses of modern social life, the manuscript is unfailingly returned to him.

If we examine the feminine types which dominate this kind of literature, we find them to be puppets arbitrarily cut and padded to conform to the established pattern. They depict woman as she should be and as she should not be, and they are plainly labelled so as to prevent any possibility of mistake.

For this family literature has an especial mission to fulfil which cannot be combined with an artistic presentation of reality. Who, then, are these "younger members of the family" who exercise such restrictive influences? Certainly not those boys who are growing up so rapidly. All this reticence about political, religious, and erotic questions is not maintained on their account. Not for them is the romantic tale prepared, the pleasant ending, rose-coloured, sentimental and unreal. Indeed, why should it be? Already at school there has been opportunity enough for them to learn in some degree the stern realities of life. You have but to look through the leaves of any favourite journal written for the "family" and you will soon see who plays the leading part. Never is the youth of eighteen the hero

female stagnation:

or the central figure of the story. His joys and sorrows do not form the themes for writers of this literature; if he appears at all it is merely to play a comic part. No! Behind this family bugbear who seems to rule so despotically, there stands no one but the young girl! And she it is for whose mental innocence the family is always trembling, and for whose eighteen-year-old intelligence all literary food must be adapted ere it can find a place upon the family table. Yes, for the girl of eighteen years, for at that age the well-bred young ladies of middle-class society are supposed to have done with their intellectual development.

The next ten years, during which a young man makes such a great stride towards maturity and independence of thought and judgment, remain unfruitful for a girl unless she happens to marry. She is considered as "finished" and grown-up from the very moment when she is first brought out in society, and the single woman of twenty-eight has no official precedence over the young girl of eighteen. On the contrary, the older woman must of necessity strive constantly to resemble the younger one as much as is possible both in mind and body.

So long as the chief aim in the training of the female is to keep her in an immature state of development for a future husband, such stagnation will be a natural result of this error of principle—an error which extends its baneful influence far beyond her unmarried years and often throughout her entire life. When she is married she enters upon new duties and new occupations; the abundant leisure possessed by a girl of the well-to-do middle class, and the opportunities she has for study, are appreciably diminished. That is why the average correct and well-bred woman remains all her life on the same mental level as in her girlish years. Her taste and her outlook in literary matters undergo no change, unless the position and education of her husband are able to exercise some influence on her mental development.

Now it is precisely the female sex which forms the most receptive, the most eager, and the most numerous class of reader. That is proved by the prosperity of all the family journals, so far greater than that of the best and most liberal periodicals. Family literature really means woman's literature. When the famous Danish author, Jacobsen, published his first novel, he wrote to Edward Brandes: "It may be that the watchmen of the people have already banned the book, and declared that it is not fit to be placed in the hands of young girls; if that is the case, it will be a failure now and for all time."

The relations of men and women to one another form the most important theme in family literature, as is quite natural when the readers are mostly women. But it is not marriage, that difficult and complicated relationship, so full of conflict, and so decisive in its influence upon a woman's life, that constitutes the chief theme, but love and betrothal. It is inevitably a pair of lovers who are brought through "exciting complications" and the most varied impediments to the "happy ending" of marriage. As soon as the affair has reached that point, the author takes leave of his readers with the comforting assurance that the wedding day is the crowning glory of life and the joyful ending of all troubles and disappointments. Only when he is very thorough in his work does he once more at the conclusion raise the curtain for a moment, to show us the young wife wrapped in ecstasy and bliss with a six-weeks-old infant on her lap.

"'The education of well-bred women," says Nietzsche, "is wonderful and monstrous; all the world has agreed to bring them up as ignorant as possible '*in eroticis.*'" The most wonderful feature of this system, however, is that the female imagination is continually stimulated with erotic matters, and the most monstrous that these erotic subjects should always be treated in a false and deceitful manner when offered as food for the female imagination. In this way the most painful wounds and disappointments are prepared for the credulous and innocent. Considering the overwhelming importance of marriage to a young woman of the middle class, her education ought to furnish her with at least sufficient knowledge and the requisite capability necessary for forming a reasonable judgment about it. But our customs have now come to such a point that they are absolutely absurd. They prescribe for a girl an ignorance and unfamiliarity with the world which were, perhaps, important conditions in days when the parents still chose the husband, and when the relations between married people were settled by social rather than by personal considerations. But now in the eyes of civilised nations it has become almost a moral postulate that the personal inclinations of those who are to be married should be taken into account. Even royal marriages, which are notoriously arranged for reasons of state, are publicly represented as being marriages of affection. A complete ignorance of life is incompatible with ability to form a personal decision respecting a bond which is to last a lifetime. It would be no exaggeration to ascribe to family literature a chief part of the responsibility for unhappy marriages, although divorce, to be sure, never comes within its range of vision. But a literature which is essentially false and deceitful, which is subservient to unwholesome and unpractical prudery, cannot fail to lead astray the imaginations of those for whom it is the only permissible mental food. By continually occupying the minds of its readers with "enthralling" romances, that is to say, with novels in which the natural course of life is twisted arbitrarily in order to produce striking effects, it has in itself a corrupting influence, weakening their power of judging ordinary people and commonplace events. The romantic method of representing love affairs also stimulates extravagantly those high-flown expectations of happiness in married life which are so great a danger and source of weakness for all young women.

Fiction is not the only department of family literature which contains these dangerous elements. Among the approved family books of that type which "may with a clear conscience be put into the hands of any young girl," we find very many that are calculated to produce exceedingly harmful misapprehensions. One example will suffice—and it is one that is honourably distinguished from the common run by its lofty tone and strong feeling—I mean *Woman,* by the French author Michelet. He himself declares in his preface that he has left gaps in the work, since he has not dealt with prostitution or with adultery. Thus, it is one of those cautious and guarded books conveniently suited to the requirements of the family table. Woman's life is described with all that fantastic sentimental exaggeration with which it is so frequently pictured in the

imaginations of men with strong passions but noble
character.   What nonsense do we encounter here!
Modern education ought to strive to make the boy a
" worker " and the girl a " religion."   " Woman is a
religion. . . . She is the flame of love and the flame of
the hearth; . . . in one word, she is the altar."   She is
the embodiment of everything that is tender, holy, and
perfect, far removed from all the sordid cares and necessities of life.   Every morning and every evening she
should pray, " Oh, God! make me beautiful."   Man,
on the contrary, is a " Herculean toiler " who from
his early youth should inure himself to all the storms
of life.   For him nothing is too rough, nothing is too
hard; and he must bear bruises in body and in soul.
For that is how women would have him be; they want
" a good pillow, on which they may trustfully lay their
heads, . . . and thus they make no sacrifice when they say,
' he is my lord and master '—and their smiling signifies :
' But I will be the mistress.' "   Thus we see that such a
" truly womanly " young lady can accomplish everything; free from all cares and fears she achieves the
most astonishing results.   " She it is who in her seven-
teenth year may by a noble word so elevate a man as to
inspire him to say : ' I will be great.' "   Michelet even
expects the man of her choice to transform himself from
" an ordinary student, the son of an ordinary citizen,
into that kingly, heroic being " of whom she has always
dreamed.   And this " transformation must be decisive
and complete," not merely during his courtship and
his honeymoon, but lasting for the remainder of his
life.

This is the sort of guidance which a well-bred young
lady receives from her spiritual counsellors and leaders.

Why should we laugh at those silly illusions of the girlish mind which lead her to believe that love will change every suitable candidate for her hand into a hero and a prince, as in the fairy stories or in her own sweet dreams? Is it possible that anyone except a maiden of seventeen would believe in sober earnest that an "ordinary citizen's son" will, after his marriage, be anything else than—the son of an ordinary citizen?

Why should young girls be thus intentionally deceived? Why should they be filled with such miserable illusions for the sake of preserving their "innocence" and their "poetic nature?"

We have not far to go when seeking the reason of this apparently benevolent deception, which is, in truth, so inexcusable. A certain type is thought to be desirable, and to this type the individual is sacrificed. Her own personal interests in life are not regarded; they are subordinated to a higher aim. She must be fitted for the marriage market, in which the traditional "ideal womanhood" has the best chances. And family literature affords the most effective means for suggesting and producing this sort of womanhood.

It has been whispered that many of these well-guarded maidens do not restrict themselves to these official precepts, but secretly extend their knowledge of the world by reading forbidden books. That is as it may be. It is certainly not easy for any single individual to break that iron band which the prejudices of good breeding have welded about the female intellect. Can anyone imagine that there could be any beneficent educational influence in such indiscriminate reading of forbidden books, even if none of them should happen to be bad?

Thus, the young girl has become a hindrance and a danger for the mental life of the nation, at least so far as real literature is concerned. In what way? Is she more responsible for this than for the other rules and regulations of good breeding? Are there not other social powers desirous that she should be trained as she is by this false literature?—powers which admire this type of woman and decree which women are to be thus disciplined?

As a mental factor in a nation's life the female sex is not so unimportant and ineffective as these powers appear to imagine. Those who look upon the struggle of women for a masculine education as the mere hobby of a few, or as a part of the general woman's movement, forget the intimate connection of every " culture movement " with the whole domain of culture. They are blind to the importance of women as consumers of literary works. The history of the development of family literature shows plainly that just in the measure in which women's training has lagged behind the training of the men, that hiatus in literature has arisen, producing that monstrous abnormal growth in the intellectual life of the nineteenth century. This symptom of profound organic disturbance will be removed only when the underlying evils have been cured.

THE CANON OF IDEAL WOMANHOOD

WE shall be able to know what women are only when we no longer dictate to them what they should be. It is, indeed, difficult to ascertain the true contours of a woman's individuality beneath the conventional exterior which the cultured woman wears like some skin-tight covering. Accustomed to a constant repression of every opinion upon life, bound by a thousand invisible threads more securely than by chains, forced by the tyranny of prevailing standards into self-deception and a fear of confessing their own divergent emotions—they silently pursue those paths which have been prescribed for them by a stronger will.

Opinions with respect to what woman "ought" to be are the determining factor of feminine education, the sole purpose of which is to suggest a fixed type to the growing girl. To be sure, the development of young men is subject to a similar influence; but as women are trained merely for one purpose, for one vocation, there is much less play for individuality within the limits of female education. In addition to this, women are generally much more disposed to subordinate themselves to authority—the fact that they are considered the weaker sex is, in the main, due to their susceptibility to suggestion. The disciplinary measures by means of which human beings are converted into "useful" members of society react more strongly upon them than upon men.

According to Laura Marholm, neither the best nor the worst of the raw material of womankind is capable of being led or trained, but only the second-rate; according to another point of view, less extensively disseminated, it is precisely the most excellent women, the "true," or "fine," women, who are most docile and adaptive. In whatsoever way we may elect to judge them, it is nevertheless true that the majority of women conform to the dominance of certain ideas with regard to their duties, in order to approximate as closely as possible to some model, some canon of womanhood. The closer they resemble this disciplinary ideal, the more womanly they believe themselves to be, and they fear to lose this womanly quality by any divergence from this ideal.

John Stuart Mill speaks of the "excesses of self-denial which form the present artificial ideal of the feminine character," and in testing the articles of faith of womanhood, one encounters a number of purely negative traits which are elevated to the rank of moral rules. Is it necessary to consider these as expressions of woman's nature? Or do they originate from without, prescribed, perhaps, for the female sex by some alien and mightier will?

That conception which has hitherto determined the social status of the female sex has decreed to woman only a secondary significance. According to this, woman is only a means to an end: first, for man's gratification; secondly, for the reproduction of man, who is in himself the final end of all the contrivances of Nature as well as of the State. No intrinsic worth as a self-sufficient personality, or a self-justified individuality, is granted to woman. She is of value only to the extent in which she serves as a means, and the only condition which morally and practically justifies the existence of woman, is marriage.

This conception, systematised philosophically and based upon the *Nature of Reason*, is to be met with in Fichte's *Basis of Natural Right according to Scientific Principles.* There we may read : " According to natural disposition, the second sex occupies a place a degree lower than the first. . . . Woman does not appertain to herself, but to man. . . . The concept of marriage decrees the unlimited subjection of woman to the will of man. . . . Her own worth depends entirely upon the condition that she belongs to her husband in all that she is, and that without a single reservation she gives herself wholly into his hands. The least of the consequences of this is contained in the law that she resign all her rights to him and follow him. Only when united to him, only in his eyes and in his affairs, does she possess life and activity. She has ceased to lead the life of an individuality."

But it is especially characteristic that Fichte has described the chief natural urging of woman as an urging to " be the means for the end of another, because she cannot be her own end without yielding up her main purpose, the dignity of reason."

This entire method of deduction, as well as the justification of the prevailing laws and morals by means of abstract principles of reason, compels us to ask : What is this element which here, under the name of " the dignity of reason," excites such a dominant and arbitrary influence? Why is this conception supposed to be symptomatic? Is it not only the instinct of a certain kind of masculinity which would legitimatise itself? Most men in their relation to woman are moralists. They are not content with justifying their demands upon woman by basing these upon their own tastes and inclinations, nor with living out their lives in an individual relation with some woman adequate to their natures; but they will tolerate no divergence from that law which is the result of their own choice, and will punish all such divergences with their personal disapprobation, stigmatising them as "degeneration" of the one legitimate normality. "True" womanhood is built up out of the wishes and necessities of such men; they have created the conventions according to which all that is feminine ought to shape itself. It is difficult to recognise in the ideas which lie at the bottom of this convention the negative form of all that arises from the demands of a definite masculine nature.

That ironic definition of Arne Garborg's: "Womanhood is the summary of all the peculiarities and idiosyncrasies, the advantages and the faults which make woman desirable unto man," proves how closely this convention is associated with the abstract idea of womanhood. There are two challenges or demands which call for special consideration here. They appear under various terms, but, analysed according to their general nature, one might describe them as beauty and as weakness. It would be impossible among all the orthodox advantages pertaining to ideal womanhood to find one which could not be placed into one or the other of these two categories.

The most unassailable of the many formulas which convert woman's beauty into a law, has been given us

women/beauty/
aesthetics:

by Neufville: "Beauty is the mission of woman: she exists under no other condition." A milder interpretation declares that grace and beauty constitute the genius of woman, or that esthetics with woman takes the place which ethics occupies with man. It is this custom of regarding the female sex as primarily the esthetic one that gives rise to all those preconceptions that pledge woman to be "a mirror of seemliness" (Julius Düboc), and also the representative of that which is known as "the grace of moderation," preconceptions which prove plainly that they are not derived from the aboriginal nature of woman. For the peculiar power of a quicker reaction to physical and psychical stimuli which one is accustomed to ascribe to the nervous system of woman, disposes her to a more violent display of their emotional effects, and for this reason annuls that repression which is demanded by the "grace of moderation."

Into the category of weakness we must place all those peculiarities which are calculated to arouse an appearance of helplessness, subjection, and dependence. The determining factor here is marriage, this being the one solitary vocation for which woman is prepared by her education. Since the prevailing ideas of marriage mean an entire resignation of a woman's personality, it must be assumed that the most docile, the most yielding, and the least self-reliant woman is best qualified for it. In this relation the forms of education are based upon a sort of law of averages. It is not the noblest, most distinguished, or most modified type of manliness which here sets up the standards, but the most ordinary, the most commonplace and familiar—in fact, just that very type with which we have to reckon.

This kind of masculinity will also be best suited by

average qualities, by the utilitarian, the pliable, by everything that possesses the cheapest qualities of agreeableness.   Only a weak being can easily and consciously subordinate itself.   Adaptation, self-surrender, lack of self-reliance, are coincident phenomena of a feeble will. Women are not only weak of will, but they "ought" to be so.   It is one of man's favourite illusions that woman first receives her personality from him. Nietzsche confirms it in these words: "Man makes himself an image of woman, and woman shapes herself to this image."   Michelet, in his book upon love, declares: "You must create you wife—it is her own wish.   We men are artizans, creators, builders —true sons of Prometheus.   We do not desire a ready-made Pandora, but one whom we ourselves create."

Here, even more plainly than in the formulas of Fichte, the subjective erotic phantasy betrays itself the origin of this assumption.   The idea that a being with definite and inborn characteristics—and even the weakest-willed woman comes under this head— could be "created" in an arbitrary fashion, does not arise from real observation, but belongs to those numerous illusions which arise in the psycho-sexual relationships of man.   Nevertheless, the methods of feminine education voluntarily foster these illusions.   In order to give an air of probability to this idea of "creating," it is necessary that girls remain undeveloped, ignorant, and even impersonal creatures until such time as they may find their "creators."   The entire procedure of feminine education is devoted to the retardation of an independent process of development; it is a method of suppression, of intimidation, of artificial prevention of growth. The well-bred girl is intimidated to such a degree that she is fearful of taking the slightest step on her own account; her way to the hallowed haven of marriage is like running the gauntlet between numberless possibilities of giving offence, of doing something that "is not proper." The fear of doing something improper exerts so powerful an influence upon the feminine soul merely because at its background lies the conception of ideal womanhood—of that paragon from which all divergence is considered as degeneration.

Since this particular ideal of education is the result of the erotic pretensions of a definite type of masculinity, since the dominant taste of a majority has created this ideal, why, indeed, should one object to it? Perhaps the female sex, because of its weakness of will, which usually creates a feeling of dependence and a need of being guarded, must, after all, be treated as a secondary sex. Perhaps it is impossible to consider it from any other viewpoint than that of its fitness for the purposes of the male? No one will deny that such happiness as arises from a perfect union between man and woman is to be considered as one of the greatest, if not absolutely the very greatest, blessing of human life. Is it not, therefore, to the interests of women themselves that they submit to all that prepares and trains them for this purpose? Should they not be content, for the sake of this treasure, to remain weak and dependent creatures for ever?

But are we here considering those lofty gifts of love which are the inevitable fruits of a consummate reciprocity? There are endless possibilities of erotic attraction, and every real love-union is built upon individual

characteristics, and not upon conventional ideas. It is
the individual nuances which determine the erotic
attractiveness—all those countless shadings of personality which decree that a man is to be moved to love
by a certain feminine individuality, and not by a
complex pattern of femininity.

In criticising the method of woman's education it is
not necessary to begin with the right to a free personality—it is merely necessary to ask whether such a
right may be demanded by women as a matter of justice.
For the rights of personality are not granted; they are
usurped; one does not wait until they come from without, one seizes upon them because of an inner necessity,
nor is there the slightest danger that education will in
any way injure strong feminine personalities.

The weaker individualities who are unable to assert
themselves or to execute their wills are far less fortu-
nately situated. But even they must be considered
from some other viewpoint than that of a secondary
sex. The more that they happen to be " merely
woman " the more significance the so-called natural
calling of woman will possess for them. One should,
no doubt, be permitted to ask just how far the prevailing ideals of feminine education are calculated to make
those who subject themselves to them capable of
fulfilling this calling.

It must be clear that a system of education which
seeks to qualify the female sex for its natural destiny,
must first of all prepare it, both mentally and physically,
for the duties of motherhood. Through maternity,
Nature has given to the female organism the most important function in the life of the species; a heavy task
which, above all things, demands a hardening of body

and of soul, fearlessness, inner courage, and a heroic disregard of physical pain. But it is in vain that we seek these qualities among the canons of "ideal" femininity. The hothouse methods of good breeding which turn woman into a mere object of luxury, thus atrophy those very tendencies and instincts which are part of motherhood; the system is one of mere pampering and softening of body and soul. How little physical resistance for the task of motherhood is possessed by the women of well-to-do classes is shown most plainly by the circumstances that so many of them are unable to bring their first child into the world without resorting to an operation, and that an act which under natural conditions occasions a suffering of only a few hours becomes with them a martyrdom of several days.

But intellectually they are still worse equipped for that which is meant to be the chief purpose of their lives. Ignorance—that mental corollary of physical virginity —since all knowledge which tends to arouse independent desires and judgments must be considered as something inimical to the condition of good breeding—this ignorance of natural functions develops a dark dread, a cowardly and timid feeling which is directly calculated to disturb and vitiate the life-instinct. For the sake of a mere imaginary advantage, well-bred girls are robbed of that inner sense of security which comes from an insight into the processes of Nature, and from that identification with her which must, especially for the female sex, possess the force of a strong religious conviction. They do not learn to love Nature as the great Mother whose care it is to protect them even in their darkest hours, but to fear her as a shadowy monster which, draped in imaginary terrors, lies lurking in their path.

In a still less degree could a life chiefly occupied with the cultivation of beauty produce a state of mind conducive to maternity.   Maternity constitutes one of the most violent attacks upon beauty : it produces not only a temporary disfigurement, but frequently a lasting one. It is precisely because their beauty is so transitory that woman should be loath to enact the *rôle* of the fair sex —since by this they doom themselves to being valued at their full worth for only a small fraction of their lives.

No; if maternity were the decisive factor in the education of the female, neither the element of weaknesses nor of beauty would occupy the first place in a valuation of womanhood.   If we glance behind the curtain of good-breeding, we behold the power which dangles the dear little marionettes to and fro—the will of man, which would find its subjective necessities materialised in the woman.

It is the " strong hand " which governs here.   And if women care to achieve the right of a free personality for themselves, or even if they desire to be trained in a more efficient manner for their so-called natural vocation than is possible under the modern ideas of good breeding, they must learn to regard the canon of ideal womanhood as that which it really is—not an ethical ideal, but a sexual one, and by no means so noble in origin as it would seem.

ON THE SUBJECT OF THE "STRONG HAND."

IT is remarkable that down to our own times women have taken part in every movement which has had for its aim the emancipation of the down-trodden and the amelioration of their lot, and have done so side by side with men and on an equality with them so long as the matter remained at issue, but that, as soon as the struggle was over, the victory won, and a party formed, they have had to withdraw into the background again.

The most conspicuous historical example of this is offered by the evolution of Christianity. In spite of the idea of the equality of the sexes which is inherent in the basic principles of Christianity, in spite of the share taken by women in propagating the faith and in braving martyrdom for it, the position of woman in the Germanic-Christian world was not substantially altered, at least, not so far as the laws were concerned, from what it had been in the world of Pagan Rome. Women were scarcely better off under the new order of things than under the old, even though during the days of persecution they had defended their creed with the same courage and self-sacrifice as the men. We have a bad precedent here, and women have every reason to reflect upon this question: Why it is that men regard them as their equals only when they are fellow-sufferers under the yoke?

But we must begin with the inquiry : <u>What sort of man is it who will have nothing in common with women, who will not suffer her to enjoy the same rights as himself?</u> For the men who suffer for a cause, and the men who carry it through to victory, are of very different types of being, and this difference is not without its influence upon the attitude which they adopt towards woman. Very few of them are able to distinguish between their own subjective taste, and the demands of an objective fitness of things. They set up as a model for the entire sex those qualities which they personally most need and court in a woman.

This is true only of men of a certain pronounced type—men masterful in love. <u>It is an unfortunate thing, only too noticeable, that, in the circles of the woman's movement, man is often indiscriminately abused.</u> <u>Yet women ought certainly never to forget all that they owe to the goodness, the magnanimity, and the sense of justice of individual men.</u> If these individual men were unable to convert the world at large to their own attitude towards women, that has been because they were unable to prevail against the majority—just as has been the case with those individual women who have stood forth above the ordinary level of their sex.

<u>The sexual relationship for the masterful man is bound up with the idea that woman is a lower order of being, essentially different from man but created for his purposes.</u> The sexual relationship ministers to his sense of superiority—it gives him the sensation of power and possession. He cannot think of woman except as belonging to him and dependent upon him.

He recognises her only in so far as she is an expedient. As a separate individuality like himself, with aims of her own, she does not exist for him.

It may be said, therefore, that the position of the female sex in life is established in accordance with the sexual instincts of the domineering type of man. The general ideas to which the female sex is expected to conform furnish an unmistakable revelation of the kind of man whose needs and desires they practically express.

Masterfulness in love manifests itself in low types of men and in lofty types, quite independently of intellectual or ethical qualities, though perhaps in somewhat different forms. Within the confines of European civilisation it has lost its full force; even the most masterful of Europeans is not to be compared with the Asiatic in his bearing towards woman. It is in the East that masterfulness in sexual relations is encountered in its extremest form, and atrocious customs, such as the sewing-up of women among the tribes living near the Red Sea, disclose the hideous state of perversity to which it sometimes leads.

In Europe, in the temperate zones of humanity, the most primitive type of the masterful man is the wife-beating husband. In his case the masterful impulse, which on a higher plane finds its vent in intellectual spheres, takes the form of physical ill-treatment; the "strong hand" is here to be met with literally, and not merely as a figure of speech, and the woman of primitive instincts does not rebel against it.

This is the type of woman in whom—not looking at the matter merely from the feminist point of view—the masterful man finds his justification, for her sexual instincts are all in the direction of self-surrender and

submission, even to the point of self-effacing slavish-
ness, thus corresponding entirely with his instincts of
mastery and superiority. Is it not natural for a man
whose cravings are for a weak, submissive, clinging wife,
to satisfy his own sexual instincts according to his inherent need? For the "real woman," he will always
be the "right man." Indeed, when the great despots,
the men of action and of invincible will, adopt this
masterful attitude in love, they are, after all, only
practising upon women what they practise in every
other field of life. The "strong hand" which they use
towards women they use in all the contingencies of life.
They ride rough-shod over the world as well as over
their wives, and they sacrifice their weaker fellow-men
to their own ends. In this type of men masterfulness in
love is the more easily comprehended in that it is consistent with their whole personality. Moreover, they
compensate their dependents for their tyranny over
them by the protection they afford them and by the
generosity which so often accompanies their strength.
Towards women these men are often not lacking in
chivalry—as may be noted in many instances in the
career of Napoleon, the greatest of all the despots of
modern times.

Relationship with the female sex would appear impossible to most such men of the higher masterful order
without some element of chivalry, and with them the
"strong hand" becomes in due course the "helping
hand" without which they imagine that women could
not stand alone in this rough world. Thus it happens
that they would be loth to forgo some measure of
gallantry in their attitude towards the sex. It would be
ungracious to insist upon their own superiority over

beings whom they consider inferior to themselves.
Therefore they devise a kind of social form in which
the semblance of subjugation effects a compromise with
the feeling of superiority, a game in which strength and
weakness seem to change places; but which, being only
a game, does not really endanger their masculine
supremacy.

But this is a game which they play only with those
women to whom they are not drawn by the full force
of their nature. What such a masterful love really
signifies, when in earnest, only the wife in the first
instance can reveal, and, as a generalisation from subjective needs to objective moral demands, " woman "
as a sex.

The masterful man's first requirement from a woman,
if he is to look upon her with respect, is that she should
exercise severe self-restraint in sexual matters; he would
rather have her quite cold than that she should show
signs of sexual emotion akin to his own. He cherishes
the idea that the woman offers herself up as a sacrifice,
even when surrendering herself to a man she loves
(Lombroso); that wives and mothers who are innately
virtuous experience only the faintest desire in regard to
a man, and sacrifice themselves in fulfilling their conjugal duties even with a husband whom they love
(Jentsch); that a woman cannot acknowledge her sexual
needs without losing her self-respect (Fichte), and so on.
To the man of higher order and finer sensibility this
idea of the dutiful but reluctant self-surrender of the
wife is unbearable, but it flatters the sexual instincts of
the masterful man. He will not accept the surrender
as a gift willingly bestowed, but prefers to regard it as
tribute enforced by his stronger will. He thinks of a

woman only as being at his disposal. It was a man of very different temperament who first spoke of a woman as "bestowing her favour" upon him.

The preference for coldness in women would seem to have its origin in the law of contrast which plays so great a *rôle* in sexual attraction. The masterful lover lacks "that fine manly tenderness which should make a man cherish the self-respect of the woman he loves and guard her against himself" (Jacobsen); the strength of his sexual desire, over which he has ordinarily no control once it is awakened, leads him to look for resistance in the woman. Instinctively he turns to the type of woman whose passivity corresponds with his aggressiveness, and thus is supplied with the balance which he himself lacks.

The disproportionately high estimation in which virginity is held arises from similar feelings. It is always the masterful lover who allows himself so much freedom in his sexual relations, who, in choosing a wife, sets such store by untarnished virginity of mind and body, and who has no forgiveness for what is called a "slip" on the part of the woman before marriage, even though it may have been in the nature of the most genuine self-sacrifice. Hence it occurs that the bourgeois code of morals lays more weight on the cultivation of innocence than on anything else in the education of young girls—or, at least, on the cultivation of ignorance, that very illusory substitute for innocence.

For the woman without sexual experience corresponds best with the masterful man's theory that sexual feelings are foreign to the sex. In her, too, he seems to see that guarantee of faithfulness which, fettered by his subjective ideas of woman, he is unable to discover elsewhere. According to the masterful man, a weak, inferior creature, without individuality—such as the woman of his conception—can have no control over herself; she is bound to succumb to temptation once she comes under the power of a masculine will. The idea of fidelity in fulfilment of a plighted troth has no place in his picture of woman; he can believe only in that fidelity which is of his own contriving—the fruit of his watchfulness, his foresight, his distrust. His relationship with his wife is always in danger in his eyes, and he keeps a jealous eye on all strangers. Hence all those barbarous decrees of the paternity laws—all those enactments which hand the wife over to the husband as though she were an ignorant child, so that he may guard the exclusiveness of his property.

According to the psychology of the masterful lover, the wife will always be the bondwoman of the man. For those who feel as he there has never been any doubt as to the right of a husband to kill a wife who has been unfaithful to him; and the fight caused by jealousy—that primitive method of sexual defence which is common also to male animals—is only another expression of that sense of ownership upon which are founded the sexual relations of the masterful lover.

What makes it necessary to combat this form of masculinity is the state of terrorism which it involves, and which bears most hardly upon the higher order of cultured women. For this type of man shuts his eyes to the existence of any other kind of woman than that of which he has need—a position based upon the notion that all women are of a piece, and are scarcely distinguishable one from another. " One woman is so like another," Max Nordau asserts, " that if you know one, you know all, with a few exceptions." The similarity between all women is one of the chief articles of faith in the masterful man's knowledge of the sex; and this view is so widely accepted that we must look upon it as a very noteworthy advance in feeling when a man says, "What does a man know about women? How many women can he ever really get to know?" It is a thousand to one that the man who speaks thus does not belong to the class of the Masterful Lover.

It is in the feelings of mastery that the illusion of understanding the whole sex finds its origin. Would it not prove one of the most deep-going influences for conversion possible for him to encounter, were the masterful lover to become acquainted with even a small fraction of the female sex? So long as he thinks he knows all women he may flatter himself that he rules them all, at least by his knowledge; but would not those who stand outside his sphere of knowledge also stand out against his superiority?

Hence, he is neither competent to formulate in his mind a manifold and comprehensive idea of womankind, nor is his own hard, unmalleable nature susceptible of an inner approach and a mingling of soul. So he finds everywhere the one type of woman which he knows. There is nothing he is so unwilling to admit as that there are exceptions to this one type. He prefers to designate as pathological anomalies all aspects of womanliness that do not accord with it. A woman who seeks independence, a woman of strongly-marked individuality, is in his eyes either a neurotic or else a mass of affectation; and he always detects the influence of a man in anything that a woman happens to achieve in the field of the intellect. Nothing that women of mark can

do or say alters his attitude in the least; the only effect
is to arouse his anger, his wrath, or his mockery. Thus
it was that Nietzsche was not ashamed to talk about the
"corruption of the instincts " in the case of women
who wished to emulate Mme. de Staël or Mme. Roland
or George Sand; and he declared that "among men
these are merely the three absurd women and nothing
more," although George Sand exercised extraordinary
influence over many eminent men, and in their eyes
certainly could not have been an "absurd woman."

Such men are not to be moved to sympathy or appre-
ciation even by the sight of the increased burdens and
troubles assumed by the woman who elects to follow the
intellectual life—burdens greater than those of the man
for many reasons. He recognises no bonds of kinship
with her through her lot being similar to his or by
reason of feelings and experiences common to both.

On the contrary, this very similarity irritates him,
for he regards as insupportable the idea of a woman
being akin to him. Such an idea, to his mind, is contrary to nature. When he sees a woman contending
against the same troubles and anxieties which he himself
experiences as a natural consequence of his intellectual
activities, he regards her as the shocking result of
straying from the right and natural path of womankind,
and passes her by with indifference or with annoyance.

Another idea of the masterful lover which also is
clearly not the outcome of experience is to be met with
in his conviction that he may conquer every woman if he
so wishes. This illusion of being irresistible is common
even to men who seem in no way qualified, either by
personal appearance or by fortune to exercise such
remarkable powers of attraction. It must be that this

certainty arises from a sort of auto-suggestion. The
higher type of connoisseur in womankind knows, however—as Paul Bourget observes in his study of the
physiology of modern love—that he can make an impression only upon a particular kind of woman, and that
with other kinds he will have no success. This is a self-
understood matter to persons with refined sexual sensibilities. Just as with the idea of his universal knowledge of woman, so, too, the illusion that he is irresistible to the entire female sex takes complete possession
of the masterful lover. . . .

Even when he does not go to these extremes of
vanity, his feeling of superiority over women remains
unassailable. Characteristic expression of this feeling
was given by the man who said : " I have been helped
out of all the holes I blundered into in the course of
my life by the intelligence and energy of women, and
yet I can't get rid of a feeling that I am superior to
them." This feeling, in truth, is not based on rational,
easily explicable motives. For if he used his reason,
the man of the grosser average could not but realise
that he is inferior to at least those women who are
intellectually advanced. And the man above the
average cannot base any sense of superiority over
women upon the purely sexual attributes which he possesses in common with the lowest of his fellows; nor
would any attempt to base his superiority upon higher
sexual qualifications rest upon sound biological founda-
tions. The male sex does not in general stand higher
in the animal world than the female, which has just as
much to do with the transmission and maintenance of
life. The great difference between them lies only in
their respective share in the mechanism of generation.

It is to the emotional energy connected with this function that we may attribute the feeling of superiority which is peculiar to the human male as his "prerogative."

If we are to understand the significance of this feeling as a natural phenomenon, we must regard it as a sexual characteristic which qualifies the individual for the performance of his duty to the species. Thus viewed, the illusion of superiority is seen to be a device of Nature for providing the man with the necessary aggressive self-confidence required for his sexual conquest; and we note that it finds its source in that primitive order of life in which the individual is rather a propagative unit than a personality. On the higher planes of life, in which the mutual relations of the sexes take on the shape of love, we find quite other and loftier operations of the soul life which annul these teleological devices of Nature. This, of course, does not exclude the possibility of the sexual instincts remaining primitive in an individual highly organised in other respects.

So long as domineering love seems to be the expression of abounding vitality, bound up with a strongly-developed will-power, so long as he who manifests these attributes is a "complete man," containing in his being the equivalents of his masterful sex nature, this sort of love remains a natural phenomenon which must be accepted as such like any other.

But we know what happens to primitive masculinity under the influences of a high degree of civilisation. The process of disruption bears most severely upon the masterful lover. He is thrown out of balance in proportion as the measure of his power of personality falls below the claims of his sexual temperament. He can no longer in ordinary life avail himself of that "strong hand" which he relied upon in his relations with woman; he is often found to be singularly lacking in vigour and self-control. He experiences a dyscrasy, or sense of discord within him, resulting from a conflict between his sexual nature and the rest of his being, and this becomes to him a fateful menace. The man who cannot use the method of the "strong hand" in regard to life generally—this being the sole basis of mastery— cannot set himself in a right relation to the wife who lies under the spell of his amorous nature; he must inevitably disappoint her in all his conflicts with external circumstances. Between his sexual life and his career as a citizen there exists a latent contradiction which secretly is, perhaps, as great a trial to him as to the wife who is dependent upon. him.

More often, indeed, it happens that the Masterful Lover remains in a state of pleasant infatuation which blinds him to the fact that his superiority exists nowhere except in the sphere of sex. For these men woman is the best audience—she is essential to them, however high they may consider themselves above her. Their relations with women are always coloured by an element of vulgar boastfulness. However tame and feeble they may in reality be, these men love to swagger before women's eyes like stage-heroes, toying absurdly with the hilts of the swords which their arms would now be too weak to wield.

To the unprejudiced looker-on there is something very ridiculous in this which is not confined to man's intercourse with woman. And yet a certain amount of boastfulness and swagger has its place in the erotic equipment of man, for Nature has devised it as a help to him in wooing, and it is of a piece with the way in which the innocent peacock spreads his tail before his female. There is no doubt that it has its due hypnotic effect upon the women who are susceptible to that type of man. It plays the same *rôle* in men that coquetry does in women—it is, in fact, the masculine form of coquetry.

To the more highly organised type of man, whose characteristic trait is a stern self-analysis, this kind of display is repugnant, yet it will be found to exist even in him in proportion to the degree in which he is influenced by the emotion of sexual masterfulness.

We have in German literature a classical instance of the way in which this masculine tendency to swagger is viewed by even the noblest and most eminent of men when they have a slight touch of the masterful lover in their composition. This is in Schiller's *Wallenstein.* Nowhere is the contrast more conspicuous between a man's words and his actions than in this drama. Its real significance, however, lies in the fact that the element of swagger, being a natural expression of masculinity, is unintentional throughout—perhaps a survival of the elementary emotions of its author, which plumed themselves so bravely in his *Worth of Men.* On every page we have such passages as: "Think not I am a woman," or, "Be not like women who forever must return to their first word," or, "Ill agrees the wail of women with the deeds of men." As a matter of fact, the deeds of his men, who seldom care to assume the responsibility of a deed, do not justify this attitude of superiority in the least.

The fact that the scene is laid in a period in which the warlike element in man flared up for the last time before disappearing altogether, throws the weakness and womanishness of these swaggerers into greater relief. What it serves to bring home to us is the dualism inherent in the manhood of a civilised age—a manhood striving to look fierce and formidable in order to justify its need of sexual contrast.

In modern literature Strindberg's *The Father* gives another and much more instructive example of the unconscious portrayal of masculine conceit. The play may, indeed, be designated the tragedy of masculine conceit, although the author meant it to be the tragedy of fatherhood, depicting the martyrdom to which Nature herself condemns man in his capacity as father. The hero, a riding-master, who suffers all the sorrows of paternity, is not the kind of man who knows how to rule, and he himself is conscious of his lack in this respect. Nevertheless, he is always seeking to pose as master in the eyes of the women of his circle. "It is as though I were moving about in a tiger's cage," he remarks, "and if I didn't hold a red-hot iron in front of their faces, they would all rush at me the first chance they got and tear me to pieces." He does not realise that it is the red-hot iron that transforms all these quite ordinary domestic cats into tigresses. "I tolerate no encroachments on my rights, either by women or by children," he blusters; and his wife, having said that she has never seen a man whose superior she did not feel herself to be, he challenges her to deadly combat with the boastful retort: "Ah, then you shall see one who is superior to you, and in a way that you will never forget." And yet at the first show of opposition he gives way in angry impotence. Distracted by doubts as to the legitimacy of his child, he bursts into tears in front of his wife, and cries out to her, "I merely yearn for sympathy like a sick man; I put aside the symbols of my strength and crave mercy on my life." He confesses to her that he thought he had noticed her contempt for his unmanliness, and that he had sought to win her love by showing himself a man. By so doing he has spoilt everything; for his wife, who had been inclined to forgive his weakness so long as he appealed to the maternal element in her as her friend, is ashamed of him as a lover. "The mother was your friend, but the wife is your enemy."

Strindberg gets very close here to the problem of that tragic conflict which is the outcome of the dual nature, the antagonistic instincts, in the modern man. The insight of the artist, however, soon becomes darkened over by the subjectivity of the masculine personality. He leaves the problem on one side and proceeds along the lines of his own tendency. "Love between the sexes is a battle. . . ."

This conception of love as a battle is one of the distinctive signs of the masterful lover. He is blind to the fact that love in its very essence is a truce in that perpetual state of warfare which prevails throughout the world, and that no relationship between the sexes attains to love so long as it contains the element of conflict. He can think only of lording it over women. It is only because masterfulness in love seldom exists in its primitive, unadultered form that the mutual attitude of the sexes is not marked by that "eternal and hostile strain" of which Nietzsche speaks, and that the Oriental treatment of the female sex is confined to those races in which no modification of the feeling of love has taken place.

By love, as here used, is meant the emotion which permits of the fulfilling of the task of generation in a spirit of self-respect, as distinguished from lust, which is limited to a purely physical desire for sexual intercourse.

A real communion of souls between individuals of opposite sex is not possible for all temperaments. This necessitates a high development in the sphere of psychosexuality. The higher and more perfect it is, the higher, more perfect, and permanent will be the emotion. The highest development of the emotion of love involves a kind of genius.

This genius, this faculty for ideal love, stands on the highest plane of psycho-sexual development, while the masterful lover stands on the lowest, at the point where sheer sexual instinct is evolving ideas still raised but little above the most primitive emotions. There are various stages between these two planes, the great majority here, as elsewhere, occupying a middle place. If we deal here only with extremes, that is because it is only the extremes that stand out clearly, and enable us to interpret certain phenomena of life. And if we have spoken only of the genius for love as exemplified in the male sex, that is not because it is not also to be met with in the female, even though less frequently, as with other forms of genius. In the very highest order of humanity, in truth, whether we look at genius in the field of art or of morals or in any other, we shall see that the differences between the sexes tend more and more to disappear.

On the other hand, the feelings of the man with a genius for love differ so widely from those of the masterful lover that they scarcely seem to have any bond in common. If the hidden basis of man's feeling of superiority is to be found in the fact that he is able to enforce his sexual will against that of the woman, whereas she cannot enforce her will against his, we may possibly, in the last analysis, trace to this elementary cause that feeling of contrast, of aloofness, of difference in kind, which makes the man master of the woman. In love, however, the man of his own accord puts aside this innate source of strength. The development of his power of love brings with it a new faculty which changes the desire of contrast into the desire of mutual sympathy and understanding—the faculty, namely, of self-abnegation. Thus comes about that miraculous phenomenon in the soul of a man—the complete transformation of the primitive instincts, the complete reversal of his teleological nature.

The man with a genius for love approaches beings of the opposite sex with intuitive understanding, and is capable of completely assimilating himself with them. He feels towards them as though they had been his predestined affinities; his love-experiences are attended by emotions of completion, of consummation, of the liberation of his essential nature, or even by those of a mystic transfusion. The sexual life entails for him not a loss of self-respect, but the improvement and enrichment of his soul through its communion with these objects of his love.

But the genius for loving is not the outcome of a wide range of conquests; its distinctive constituents have, indeed, nothing to do with the question, any more than they are to be identified with an exclusive fidelity to one woman. Among those who have possessed it have been men like Novalis, who have devoted themselves so fully to one loved being that they have felt it to be their greatest honour to give up life itself, if death should sunder them; while there have been other polygamous natures, like Goethe, who have been able to give their love to more than one woman at a time. Nothing could give a better idea than those passages in his letters to Frau von Stein in which Goethe describes his visits to Friederika and Lilly after many years of separation. "I cannot convey to you," he writes, "the beautiful emotion which I experience. Though I am now on quite matter-of-fact terms with them, I have for them a feeling of really deep affection. There is in it a quite ethereal happiness—it is as though I had been saying a rosary of which the beads were memories of the truest, the most endurable and unextinguishable friendship."

In the bonds which unite the man who has this genius for loving with the women of his choice, there is nothing of that hostility or enmity which, in the case of the masterful lover, declares itself in the moment when the chain of sexual attraction breaks. These bonds consist in that feeling of "unextinguishable friendship" which does not end when the phase of rapture has passed.

It would perhaps be even true to say that the genius for loving finds its deepest and strongest expression in a man's relations with women, and not in his friendships with men. Richard Wagner wrote to Mathilde Wesendonk that only a loving woman could give him the comfort he needed when longing to find peace and rest in the harbourage of some human heart, and that experience had shown him that, despite many noble attempts, he could not derive this comfort from friendship with men.

The nature of the man gifted with the genius for loving shows itself in its noblest and most beautiful form in these letters of Wagner's. A limitless self-abnegation, a craving for unrestricted community of soul, are here voiced with an intimacy which is the more wonderful in that Wagner's impetuosity and forcefulness of character make him stand out as a conspicuously "manly" man. Wagner feels he cannot do enough to convince the woman he loves that he cannot live without her, that he is just as she is, that he feels as she feels, that he shares all her emotions of joy and sorrow, and that even his art is dear to him only in so far as it accords with the deep harmony that unites him to her. His real earnestness of thought did not lie in his work, but in her. "Nothing has significance, nothing has any purpose for me, save through you. . . . With you I can achieve everything, without you nothing!"

How different is this language from what the masterful lover is wont to use! And we find an astonishingly close parallel to Wagner's outpourings in Goethe's letters to Frau von Stein. The same joyful recognition of the lover's need, the same feeling of happiness in the completeness of their mutual understanding, the same unreserved surrender of self to the woman of his heart: "Yes, dear Lotte, I realise fully now for the first time how truly you are, and must ever be, the other half of my soul. I am no longer a solitary being, standing alone. Through you I have supported all my infirmities, protected the vulnerable sides of my nature, and perfected my faulty being. . . . I see how little I count for by myself, and how necessary to me your presence must ever remain, so that I may become whole. . . . I beg of you, falteringly, to complete your

work and make me good through and through; . . .
mould me and shape me in such wise that I may remain
worthy of you! "

The idea that it is the man who must mould and
shape, " forming " his wife in accordance with his own
ideas and his own will, and that she is to be indebted to
him for her entire spiritual life—an idea expressed so
frankly, for instance, in the letters of Heinrich von
Kleist to his bride—is here replaced by a conception
absolutely opposed to it: all trace of pride of sex has
gone and self-surrender has taken its place.

The inspiration derived from woman sets free the
highest gifts of the soul in the case of men who have
the genius for loving. Woman in their eyes is the
intermediary between the world of the senses and the
Godhead—as Sophie von Kühn was to Novalis; a guide
to perfection—as Beatrice was to Dante; or a dispenser
of all knowledge and all spirituality—as Vittoria Colonna
was to Michael Angelo, who wrote:

> " Out of my lips thy spirit still comes flowing ;
> From will of thine this will of mine is growing,
> And thy heart's ardours in my heart are glowing.
> Methinks my being like the moon's dependeth
> On that great light the sun of heaven spendeth,
> Which, having not, my brightness straightway endeth."

And Goethe declared the greatest influence in his life
to have been Charlotte von Stein, with Shakespeare
coming next:

> " Lida, Glück der nächsten Nähe
> William, Stern der schönsten Höhe,
> Euch verdank ich, was ich bin.
> Tag und Jahre sind verschwunden,
> Und doch ruht auf jenen Stunden
> Meines Wertes Vollgewinn."

The wealth of graceful and charming fantasies in which the genius for loving has found expression belongs to the noblest treasures of human emotion; and the literature of all races shows us how the soul of woman inspires this capacity for love when artistic genius goes with it. We may tell from the individuality and depth of the characteristics with which an author endows the women in his books to what extent the genius for loving accompanies his genius as a writer. We know the difference there is in this respect between the women of Goethe and those of Schiller; and if it must be recognised that Schiller's heroines are lacking in womanly individuality, the cause of this may be traced to his inability to realise the woman in himself. It is in this faculty that the genius for loving finds its origin, its nature being more nearly akin to, and more in sympathy with, beings of the opposite sex. In this mystery of the highest form of love the division between the sexes disappears, and there results a veritable blending of two souls.

What we find embodied in the figure of Don Juan is at the opposite pole from the genius for loving. Don Juan is merely the male conqueror, the *virtuoso* of sex —the unresting hunter of a quarry he never captures: woman. For even in its extremest form mere sexuality can never establish a communion of souls between man and woman; he who has not already found his way to the soul of a woman by some other way, will not do so through the channels of sex. Men who have in them no faculty of loving are therefore apt to declare that women have no soul. They do not know that despite all their sexual prowess they are psychologically impotent.

The masterful lover does not get rid of the disadvantages of his sexual nature any better in his capacity as an intellectual man than on the lower planes of feeling. The further he becomes removed from the primitive condition of mind in which sexual matters have not begun to be problems, the more bitter and inimical does his attitude toward woman become; it takes on a poisoned point; it rankles like a wound in his soul. He either becomes a cynic—or, much less frequently, an ascetic; and the mere blend of cynical effrontery and ascetic aversion which distinguishes the attitude of the modern man of culture towards sexual questions tends to reveal the kind of mental attitude which generally prevails.

The conflict between self-respect and sexual desire which ceases only with the coming of love, often becomes intensified in the masterful lover in proportion to his psychological growth. Regarding woman as a creature unlike himself, and far inferior to himself, he is impelled into a condition of hostility to her by that very dependence upon her which sex entails. Only when he is dominated by sex does he venture to approach her. And she attains to influence over him only by accident; she subjugates him like some strange force which delivers him into the hands of a being whom in the main he disparages and abhors. That he should be subject to this force robs him of his self-respect, and brings about a painful disenchantment when he comes back to his senses.

Thus it happens that the sexual element, which in primitive man was the source of an enhanced self-esteem and a conscious superiority, tears him in two directions by reason of the duality of his nature—a duality which is not confined to his own life, but which confronts him everywhere throughout the cosmos.

There are certain features in common which go to prove that there is a connection between the ascetic-pessimistic outlook on life and the non-erotic sexuality which accompanies a high order of intellectuality. The monstrous idea of all mankind being in a condition of ineradicable guilt through the sinfulness of the sexual act, and of the entire life of the earth as nothing more than a curse-laden illusion, would seem to have its source in the conflict which tears asunder the souls of this order of man. The great despisers of the animal life of man, the men who devised a transcendental existence in another world, were most of them at the same time despisers and antagonists of women. To the man whose conscience is troubled by reason of his sexual desires, a world which is peopled by procreation must necessarily be accursed, and woman, the eternal object of this evil desire, must be the immediate cause of the curse. It is typical of this attitude of mind that masculine fancy should represent woman as the temptress and the cause of the fall of man, and that the redemption should be made to come from an "immaculate" virgin, a woman raised above sex.

What is symbolised by the myth of Adam and Eve: the representation of the man's soul in subjection to a woman, the seduction of this soul through sexuality— that active *rôle* being attributed to the woman which in real normal life man arrogates to himself; this piece of symbolism has left deep marks throughout the entire history of civilisation. It has had practical consequences which have borne heavily upon the female sex as being intellectually the weaker half of mankind.

The advanced intellectualism of man revenges itself on woman for man's sufferings through sex. This comfounding of a subjective condition for the object which is its cause does no credit to the masculine intellect. But this is not yet the worst.

If even under normal circumstances the conceptions of the masterful lover bring forth a pronounced adverse attitude towards all those women who do not conform to them they amount to a positive peril when they grow to such an intensity as to border on the field of pathological perversity.

The term Sadism is applied to a form of psychopathic sexual aberration which consists in the attaining of emotion and gratification through cruel acts. An element of the cruel is latent always in the masterful lover, and it discloses itself in the craving to make the woman feel the weight of the strong hand, and to possess her as a creature without will, passively submitting to the sacrifice of herself. When this element grows to extremes, or becomes connected with morbid instincts, it prepares the ground for Sadic perversity. The tendency to torment the object which is sexually accentuated in the consciousness may also be given an intellectual direction. In such instances the gratification of this desire takes the form of a belittling and defamation of the female sex—something which may well justify us in speaking of an intellectual Sadism. Perhaps it is largely a masculine desire for revenge which furnishes the incentive for the slanderous literature on the subject of woman—the work of men who, in one way or another, may have suffered at the hands of women. In other cases such literary creations are doubtlessly engendered by some morbid instinct, and, in an intellectual sense, may be considered as sadistic acts. A historical document of intellectual Sadism which must be considered as of the utmost importance because of the wide influence it exerted, is the *Malleus maleficarum* —that terrible book which, filled with a superstitious rancour and a fanatical fury against the female sex, gave rise to the infamous Witch Trials. We cannot afford to ignore this work when considering the extremes of that masculine hostility which arises from a diseased sexuality, for whatever extraneous circumstances may have had to do with the origin of the "Witch Hammer," there can be no doubt that the subjective bias of the two Dominican friars who compiled it will largely explain its inspiration. All things foul and maniacal which had been conjured up since the earliest times by the sexual imagination, all that had ever been invented by a Satanic joy in monstrous sexual orgies, were gathered together by these writers in order to lay them as a burden upon the back of womankind. The history of the Witch Trials is a terrifying example of the effects which, under certain conditions, such insane ideas are able to produce. "The universal epidemic of belief in devilish sorcery and in demon-paramours, as well as the fear of witches, which caused the Christianity of Western Europe to live in fear and trembling for over two centuries, was caused chiefly by the *Witch Hammer*, which first prepared for itself the millions of sacrificial victims which it afterwards destroyed. From the time when this codex for the persecution of witches was first set up, both Church and judgment chamber toiled together in order to build up the theory, Philosophy and Medicine gave their faithful aid, and the penal laws supplied in their turn the material that went to conform the theory." (Soldan's *History of the Witch Trials*.)

When we consider that the objective signs whose grotesque explanation gave rise to the witch-mania must, in all likelihood, have been caused by that illness which is known to-day as hysteria, then, indeed, do the Witch Trials assume the shape of a shameful monument to the inefficiency of the masculine intelligence in all things wherein sexuality and the relationship to woman play a part. Even if it be assumed that not only hysterical, insane, and absolutely guiltless women were among the victims, but also numbers of depraved, malicious, and crafty women, even then do the criminal annals of the Witch Trials so greatly surpass in baseness, malice, and superstition all the possible transgressions of those punished, that the executive officers of the law appear to sink immeasurably below the level of the condemned.

According to the *Malleus maleficarum*, it was chiefly through "the insatiable lust which incites to intercourse with demons" that women became the paramours of fiends. They were also inclined to this by reason of their inferior strength of faith, for, according to the etymology of the *Witch Hammer*, the term femina was derived from *fe* and *minor*! A considerable part of the *Witch Hammer* consists of obscene details which served to embellish this idea of sexual intercourse with demons; details which suggestive questions were to wring from the victim upon the rack and which plainly prove that not only a priestly and political lust for power lay behind this work, but also a sexual perversion which, by means of imaginary abominations, satisfied a sadistic and destructive impulse directed against the female sex.

We are in general inclined to believe that all things which have been part and parcel of the past have also been done away with. Modern science has swept ancient superstition from its domain, but the dark depths of the human soul are not so easily swept clean, and it might well be that the old hostile mania with regard to woman still pursues its evil purpose in the guise of milder forms and under a more modern mask. Even to-day philosophy and medicine still serve faithfully to confer a halo of objective truth upon subjective figments of the imagination. Is it not a so-called man of science, Lombroso, who declares that "even the normal woman is a half-criminaloid being"? Is it not a matter of recent history that Weininger, with a vast display of philosophic thoroughness, endeavoured "to prove in the most comprehensive manner that woman is soulless, that she possesses no ego and no individuality, no personality and no freedom, no character and no will"—thus, in the twentieth century, answering in the negative the very question: "Has Woman a Soul?" which the Christian misogynists at the Council of Mâçon were forced to answer in the affirmative more than a thousand years ago? Mad and obscene ideas, as, for instance, "indiscriminately, every woman feels herself throughout her entire body, constantly and without exception, in a state of *coitus*" (Weininger), run closely parallel to the ideas of the *Witch Hammer* with respect to the "insatiable lust of woman," and indicate a specific psycho-sexual condition as their common source of origin, unchanged by the passage of the centuries.

This source has its ebb and flow in the history of
society.   It sinks in those fruitful eras of growth in
which gifted personalities abound, and infuse the riches
of their emotional life into the culture of the times; it
rises in the days of decline when the base, unbridled
tendencies of human nature seize the reins of power and
all manner of evils threaten the healthy life of the instincts.   Just so high as woman stood in the estimation
of man during the times of the Renaissance and the
periods which led up to it, just so deeply did she sink
during the era of the Thirty Years' War when the
ideas of the *Witch Hammer* had become common
property, ideas which the contemporaneous society of
this book had passed by without regarding.

To conclude, let us return to the starting-point of
these observations and their application.   We repeat:
a man in his relationship to other men may be as unprejudiced, as just, and as objective as possible, but if
the psycho-sexual side of his personality happen to be
of a hard, coarse, and domineering strain, he will be
incapable of thinking justly and without prejudice of
woman.   No matter how lofty a thinker he may be,
here he finds his limitations.   Ah! if women only knew
how little cause they have for smiling at this limitation
of the masculine mind!   They must pay dearly for this
very shortcoming.   Since everywhere, with the exception of England, women are in the minority as compared with men, since they are dependent upon them
because of their weaker wills and feebler intelligences,
and, in addition to this, subject to the " strong hand "
because of their erotic inclinations, the subjectivity of

man in sexual matters creates a tragic fatality which rests upon the entire female sex.

Nevertheless, those women whose natures contain more positive elements than are compatible with the demands of the domineering variety of eroticism will have to determine for themselves which men will grant them recognition and which will not. They may not in their struggles hope to convince by the power of this or that particular argument; nevertheless, it is possible that Nature herself may come to their assistance. Inasmuch as sexuality has, during the evolution of civilisation become sublimated into love, why should a biological change, destined to influence still further the psycho-sexual disposition of the sexes, be regarded as a mere Utopian assumption? It is not beyond the limits of possibility that the conditions of life imposed by a steadily growing civilisation may more and more frequently affect that particular type of masculinity which finds its loftiest expression in the man with a genius for love. These conditions of life, which constantly tend to eliminate the external differences in the activities of the two sexes, operate likewise in the sense of a constant approach and have the tendency to deprive the domineering instinct of at least its social support.

The increasing intellectualisation of humanity may likewise in course of time have the effect of inducing a greater number of men to arrive at an objective decision between the women of their erotic tastes and those who are valued without regard to sexual selectiveness. Among the domineering type of amorists there have always existed those individuals whose theoretical views of the social position of women were far more liberal

than was consistent with the practice of their private
lives.   Is it not possible that a man may publicly proclaim himself a supporter of political equality for women
and yet in his domestic relationship to his own wife
allow his domineering nature to come to the fore?   It
would be unjust to reproach such a man with inconsistency; one ought rather to recognise in his attitude a
symptom of a remarkable and infrequent elevation above
the common subjectivity, an admirable independence of
the intellect from the bonds of an elemental, intrinsic
quality.

The part taken by women in modern ideals of culture,
in the liberation of the individual for the purpose of his
unfettered spiritual development, in the battle for the
rights of a free personality, will not, in the long run,
pass without leaving its definite stamp upon the organisation of society.   Therefore the signs of a reaction
against this movement, evidenced by a growing antagonism between the sexes and in occasional outbreaks
of the masterly masculine type against the " unsexed "
or the " brainy " woman, may be assumed to have the
same symptomatic significance as the intensification of
the national and the race feeling in an epoch which
endeavours to obliterate these differences between the
races and the nations by means of its policies or its
forms.   Both phenomena indicate that an opposition
must arise in the consciousness of those whose emotional
life is not in accordance with the new conditions.

It is undeniable that the unchangeable, inherent
nature of the human being will continue to be the barrier
over which no man may make his way; nevertheless, to
a certain degree all things are capable of being taught

as well as learned. The suggestive influence of great examples signifies an element of culture of the highest value. With imperishable and luminous words the genius of love in man has for centuries proclaimed unto humanity the glad tidings that a relationship is possible between the sexes far different from any of which the men of the "strong hand" have ever permitted themselves to dream.

THE SUBJECTIVE FETICH OF SEX.

WHY is it that certain women encounter so much good fortune and others again so much evil? What treachery of fate can account for the fact that most women have nothing but a mere one-sided choice? What secret law controls the experiences from which man builds up the sum total of his knowledge of woman?

More clearly than in aught else are here manifested these two peculiarities which at root so strongly confine the spiritual life of humanity: the dependence of all thought upon inherent idiosyncrasy, and the tendency to regard the results of individual thought as objective truth. If the truth which is arrived at by any distinct and separate intelligence is always conditioned by the individualism of type, must it not also be true that the hidden relationship between so-called objective thinking and the spiritual-corporeal constitution of man is most directly operative where the question is not one of principles of abstract knowledge, but of a concrete phenomenon so intimately and personally related to man as is " woman "?

The intellectual process which takes place in arriving at a generalisation, or in combining separate data of experience into one general conclusion, is something which cannot be severed from the essence of him who experiences it—otherwise identical facts would never be so variously presented by different persons.

But even those persons who by means of an *a priori* method utter their opinions as to the " true nature of woman," or base " woman's being " upon " principles of pure reason," or even adhere to the " platonic idea of woman," must ask themselves this question : what are the original conditions which give rise to ideas such as these in an individual intelligence?—and also to what extent their own subjectivity has helped to create these general assumptions.

It was the hermit of Sils Maria, the man of " exceeding honesty," who pointed out that in matters such as these no man is able to know more than that which is already determined for him, that which is confirmed in the very depths of his spiritual constitution.

" At the very roots of our being, deep ' down below,' there lies something unteachable, the granite of a spiritual destiny, of predetermined judgments and answers. . . . For example, with regard to man and woman a thinker cannot unlearn, but merely out-learn—he can only discover to the very end that which is ' established ' in him. At times we are enabled to light upon certain solutions of problems which fortify our beliefs—perhaps thenceforward we call them our ' convictions.' Later, we behold in them mere footprints to a knowledge of self, guide-posts to the problem of ourselves—or, more correctly, to that great folly which is but another name for ourselves—to our spiritual destiny, to the unteachable elements far ' down below.' " (*Beyond Good and Evil.*)

With these remarks Nietzsche prefaces those one-sided and unjust verdicts which he pronounced upon

the female representatives of the modern women's movement, and in this wise lays special emphasis upon the
fact that it is only his own subjective taste which is here
expressed. "In consideration of this act of courtesy
which I have just committed, so to speak, at my own
expense, I trust that I may be permitted the sooner to
express certain truths with regard to ' woman as woman '
—provided that one is now aware in advance how very
much these happen to be only—my own truths."

But, long before Nietzsche, Goethe spoke these
thoughtful words to Eckermann: "Women are silver
shells into which we lay golden apples. My ideas of
woman are not obtained from the experiences of reality,
but they are inborn in me or have developed in me,
Heaven knows how."

In Grillparzer we find the dictum: "A woman—what
might it be? . . . A something which is never anything, never nothing, just as I happen to imagine it—
I—I alone." (*Fraternal Strife in Habsburg.*)

Let us, therefore, state that the position which the
individual man, both in theory and practice, assumes
with regard to woman is determined only to a slight
extent by experience; further, that the experiences which
each man undergoes are already predetermined by an
original bias in his own soul. Experiences from without
can no more alter this original bias than they could
alter the idiosyncrasies of his own type. It is not
probable that a man, irrespective of the various experiences he may undergo, will alter his opinions of the sex,
save when overtaken by a subversion of the entire
psychical self such as occurs occasionally in old age or
in sickness. The converted woman-hater is, to be sure,
a rather common character in romantic literature, but in

real life the conversion is almost as rare as that fundamental religious one which Christian faith always attributes to an act of divine grace. It is impossible to call
those men woman-haters who think slightingly of women
merely because their subjective conception of the sex
is of so lofty a nature that the great majority of women
can by no means attain to it—thus forcing such men
to seek long in vain for the realisation of their ideals.

Every individuality reacts to the distinct charms of
another. This fact, embodied in the term "subjective
taste," is almost a commonplace. Ordinary persons
whose consciousness with regard to their sexuality does
not rise far above the torpor of the instinctive life,
remain dull and apathetic to all those ideas concerning
the other sex which are based upon subjective taste.
They seize upon the conventional, that is to say, the
opinion created by the majority, and very frequently
they adhere to it even when it no longer coincides with
the experience of their lives, only because they are not
sufficiently awake to be acted upon by the reflexes of
their own personal feelings. But wherever imagination
or passion or a highly developed capacity for abstract
thought manifests itself in an individuality—as with
persons who are intellectually creative—the field of consciousness is filled with clearer and more positive forms.

That complexity of individual traits which constitutes
our own personality, which differentiates it from all
others, and which is mirrored in our consciousness as
the embodiment of our own ego—also, to a certain
extent, creates as a by-product a more or less sharply-
defined image which we project into the outer world
and endeavour to find embodied in the individuals of
the other sex. This is true equally of the male as of the

female sex.   But inasmuch as the masculine consciousness is the more communicative and expansive and gives
forth more of its contents in the shape of creative
thought, this proceeding becomes more noticeable among
men—the more so as the consequences arising therefrom
are of greater general significance in view of the authoritative rank of the male sex.

The facts of experience with regard to subjective
conceptions of " woman " furnish only the materials for
building, the plan of the building is fixed by individuality.   All the facts of experience are interpreted according to this plan—all that is observed is in this manner
and in conformity with a definite law, conceived as
typical.   Each seizes upon that which confirms his particular type and willingly enshrines it in his remem-
brance, but impressions which limit or possibly destroy
this type are considered as disturbing, restrictive or dis-
agreeable.   Frequently they are not even perceived, or
when they are perceived, vanish swiftly from the
memory.

Nothing is so significant as the air of infallible certainty which men assume in their generalisations about
" woman," even those men who, in their attitudes to
all other phenomena in the realm of experience, preserve
the most careful and conscientious reticence of thought.
This certainly proves that they confuse the empirical
woman with the immanent woman in the crudest
manner.   The empirical woman, the intrinsic individual
being of female kind, is a manifold phenomenon like
man himself, and in her multifariousness she is as in-
commensurable as he.   The immanent woman is, on the
contrary, a creature of the imagination, is known to every
man and is as familiar to him as his own ego—since it

is from this very ego that it has been produced and with which it has become incorporated.

All general judgments which a man may pronounce upon woman must first be qualified by a certain significance, manifesting itself as a symptom of his own psycho-sexual predisposition.   Such judgments have more of a biographical than a normalising value.   That which he hopes for or fears in woman, or desires and presupposes, his opinion as to what woman " should " be, furnish a rather reliable estimate of his own nature.

It is the need for completion which operates as the highest law in the psychical relation of the sexes.   In accordance with this need the particular fetich which the imagination of every person conjures up with regard to the other sex is marked by those very features which form a complement, and in some respects a reversal, of his own nature : it is something which arises in the soul like a complementary colour in the vision.

Richard Wagner, whose theoretical writings have contributed so greatly to the psychological studies of poets and musicians, gives us a remarkable glimpse into the origin of a subjective sex-fetich in *A Communication to my Friends*, wherein he describes his poem of *Lohengrin* as a symbolisation of an inner experience. The deeper meaning of this poem he declares to be the embodying of his own emotions in the figure of Lohengrin—as a yearning from the lonely heights of pure art for the lower levels of common human life.   From this height his longing vision beholds—woman. "From the very beginning I saw in Elsa that antithesis to Lohengrin which I so longed for—naturally not an absolute and remote antithesis to his own being, but rather the other part of it, that opposite which is really contained in himself and which of necessity only comprises the completion of his own peculiar masculine nature. Elsa is the unconscious, indeterminate nature in which˙ the conscious, positive nature of Lohengrin endeavours to find salvation."

How characteristic of the individuality of Richard Wagner, whose chief peril as an artist lay in doctrinal knowledge, is the fact that he believed that in Elsa's unconsciousness and indeterminateness he had surely discovered the "essentially feminine"! The preponderance of intellectual activity which constitutes such a disturbing, burdensome and obstructive element for all artistically productive persons is the thing from which he fancies he would be "saved." But since the operation of an influence so deep-going as this—assuming that it is even thinkable—can be brought about only by means of a psycho-sexual interfusion, he projects the thing he yearned for in the form of a woman—of woman in the concept of the "essentially feminine." Nevertheless, he by no means presumed to find the embodiment of this essential woman in individuals among women, or even to regard it as a norm, which would enable one in real life to distinguish the "true" from the "spurious" women.

On this point his sensibilities proved to be far deeper and richer or, one might say, juster, than those of Nietzsche, his later opponent. That Nietzsche's fetich also concealed a natural antithesis and a need for "salvation," is confirmed by the fact that even he, whose destiny was determined by an urging toward an unqualified truthfulness and honesty of thought, gave forth this formula: "Originally nothing is more alien, more antagonistic and more hostile to woman than truth—

her great art consists of falsehood, her loftiest concerns are mere appearance and beauty. Let us acknowledge it—we men: we honour and love precisely this very art and instinct of woman—we who endure much, and love to ally ourselves for our solace with those beings under whose hands, glances and tender follies our own earnestness, heaviness and profundity appear almost like another form of ' folly.' "

This glorification of feminine falsity and superficiality is a most remarkable and unusual example of sex-idolatry. Let us contrast with it the wrath and abhorrence with which suspicious and dishonest authors —especially those who themselves suffer from these qualities and would rise above them—speak of these very same feminine peculiarities and how highly they praise the innocence and deep sensibility of the " true " woman. The same attitude is adopted by the intemperate, the unbridled and depraved among men—who make a habit of regarding woman as the goddess of a fine moderation, of propriety and purity.

The dominance which is exerted over the soul of an individual by an imaginative subjective sex-fetich frequently attains the power of an obsession; but even when it does not assume this fanatical quality, it nevertheless remains one of the most potent and unconquerable of illusions. For it must not be forgotten that it stands in close relationship with the most important contingency which, with the one exception of self-preservation, occurs in human life—that of sexual selection. It is in the love-relationship˙ that the subjective sex-fetich attains to its greatest significance; there, too, one may most easily observe the blindness which it occasions.

Nothing else than this dominance in love of the

immanent woman is meant by Maeterlinck when he says: " Vainly we may elect to fix our choice on this hand or the other hand, upon the heights or within the depths; it is in vain that we strive to emerge from that magic circle which we feel is drawn about all our views of life, to do violence to our instincts, or thwart our stars by attempting to achieve an independent choice; we shall never fail to select the woman who has descended upon us from some invisible sphere.   And even should we kiss a thousand and three women, like Don Juan, we shall (at last) come to know that it is always the same woman who stands before us, the good or the evil, the tender or the cruel, the loving or the faithless.''

In his romance, *The Triumph of Death*, d'Annunzio causes this thought to pass through the mind of his hero: " She is—as she appears to me every moment to be—nothing more than the constant operation of my inner creative powers.   Outside of myself she does not exist. . . .''

Prybiszeffski, in his sultry, ecstatic style, speaks thus: " Thou wast in me ere I saw thee—thou didst lie chastely in my brain, as a prototype of immaculate purity, as an idea purely conceived, . . . then in an instant thou hadst spun the thread between my creative brain and the slumbering, brooding, animal soul of sex, . . . and thou, sex-animal, didst merge with the original image of my mind and grewest into a mighty whole.'' (*Vigils.*)

Here we encounter a note that portends evil, for surely no good is to be expected when a " sex-animal '' and a " purely-conceived idea '' merge into one.

The subjective figment of the imagination determines

the relationship between the individual man and the woman of his choice—to the happiness of those concerned when the real character of the woman approaches the fetich—but as a misfortune when the fetich unites itself to the wrong person. Among the errors which lie at the root of unfortunate love affairs, the influence of this subjective image of the phantasy occupies a considerable place. The battle between the immanent and the empirical woman is frequently visible in all its violence in those passionate reproaches and accusations, in the despairing oscillations between love and hate, which, in such cases, accompany the process of dissolution.

Strindberg, with great artistic honesty, but with a repellent pathological note, has pictured the extremes of this battle in his *Confessions of a Fool.* Out of the confusion, the inconsequence and moodiness of passion, which make their appeal to the judgment of the "enlightened reader," now by means of outbursts of fury, now by a half-fainting perplexity, there emerges first the fetich and then the real woman, according to the circumstances in which the author happens to be living. When he is seated for some time at the side of his beloved, the real person occludes the fetich and fills him with a jealous restlessness; when he leaves her, the phantasm of the pale, young woman, the mirrored image of the virgin mother " arises before him and the "picture of the unbridled comedienne " is erased from his memory. One might well imagine that this woman, under the suggestive influence of her own fetich, shows herself quite other than she really is, but as soon as she forgets her *rôle* she becomes to him an object of contempt and loathing. He makes absolutely no attempt to arrive at any clear and sufficient understanding of her real nature, even the very thought that she may be capable of sexual impulses drives him beyond reason : " Is it possible that this cold and lustful Madonna may belong to the class of born prostitutes? " There is no indignity with which he does not confront her during their union : he foams against her with treacherous malice, compares her to the spider who devours her own mate—and no sooner is he separated from her than the same game repeats itself : " The Madonna of my first dream of love rises before me, and this works upon me to such an extent that on meeting an old comrade of my journalistic days I confess that I have become humbler and purer through the influence of a noble woman."

The endless variety of feminine characteristics which, as judgments upon woman, are revealed to us in the literature of the world, also testify to the multiplicity of the fetiches which are conjured up by the masculine imagination. It is possible to classify these fetiches by groups according to the relation of rank; that is to say, the relation in which the man as a person stands to the woman as a person. Since the male sex in accordance with the external order of things is the foremost as well as the governing sex, it follows that the sexual relation of rank as reflected in the mind of the individual man assumes a special and weighty significance. In conformity with this external order of things, man must necessarily assign to woman a place beneath his own. The fetich of the bondwoman reigns in this order of things. In spite of this the fetich of a " higher being," or of a mistress which man sets above him, has played no inconsiderable part in the history of civilisation—as

the masterful/chivalrous/comrade lover:

types creating types

well as the fetich which man sets at his side—that of the helpmate. It is only the main outlines of the various relationships which are shown forth in these three figures, but they are drawn from these three groups— into which men are arranged according to their sexual natures, and which may be described as the masterful, the chivalrous, and the comrade-like.

Since the rank and worth of separate male and female individuals are purely relative, it would be possible for every man, in so far as he proceeds from an objective point of view, to discover in the world of reality such women as stand above him, and such as stand beside or beneath him. It would, therefore, seem that the ordinary man of no importance would be the first to set woman above him, and that only such men as have reached the loftiest summits of human perfection, which hitherto no woman has attained, would have the right to regard woman as beneath them. But the very opposite is the case. The lowest and most miserable fellows usually imagine themselves superior to woman, and manifest their tyrannous self-esteem in brutal or malicious acts; while, on the contrary, many of the noblest and most distinguished men think of woman as a spiritual mistress or a consort, thereby creating a dream-figure which transcends reality.

According to the depth and richness with which the amorous side of a person's nature is developed, even so rich and individualised will be the figment of the imagination which the other sex will inspire in that person. A needy, inflexible, one-sided eroticism is incapable of projecting a complete or harmonious image of woman; it will at best be equipped with very general, very superficial qualities of sex; and, at the worst, with mean or negative qualities, without substance—an empty sheet on which man must first inscribe his will.

The image of the bondwoman, the subjective sex-fetich of the domineering lover, is the oldest, the most widespread, and the most vulgar, and determines the position which the female sex occupies, if not in the social scheme, then at least before the law.

When the bondwoman happens to encounter her complete antithesis in the idea of the mistress, the idol of the knightly type of eroticism, then, remarkable as this inversion may appear, there nevertheless occurs no essential change in the degree of strangeness that exists between the sexes. The idea of womanly weakness which sways the mind of the domineering man, is the very same as that which determines the idol of the chivalrous man, though in the latter it is combined with the idea of the moral ascendancy of the woman, and necessitates that the lord and master become the servant and the protector who takes pleasure in his voluntary subordination so long as he may feel himself a protecting power.

Yet the conception of a vast and insurmountable sex-difference lies deep at the very heart of the knightly ideal; it is, like the fetich of the masterful man, rooted in a need for an antithesis; it differs only in the direction in which it operates. This ideal cannot be maintained without preserving a certain remoteness between the holder of it and the person upon whom it is centred—for which reason Nietzsche declares, "The magic and the mightiest power of women is . . . a power in the distance, *an actio in distans*; but for this one must, first and foremost, have—distance."

The most celebrated figures which the chivalrous fetich has ever created—Dante's Beatrice and Petrarch's Laura—do not belie this idea of distance; and through this they give inspiration to that especial domain of the knightly idolatry—poetry, which of all things is least adapted to come into touch with reality—whereas, on the other hand, the domineering amorist who, devoid of all romance, wins his ideas from the clay of common, everyday life, has shaped woman to suit his own notion of domestic usefulness.

Perhaps the only idol or ideal which in itself contains a real basis for a true understanding, a real approach between man and woman, is the ideal of the mate, the subjective idea that woman stands neither above nor below man, but beside him in human communities wherein the sexual differentiation has as little to do with intellectual as with physical superiority. This ideal is frequently attacked, especially by the defenders of the masterful type of amorist, as a feeble invention of modern feminine thought, or even as a product of deterioration, since it exists only since the days of the French Revolution. It is in reality of a far more ancient origin than this; some of the most glorious spirits of antiquity, such as Plato and Plutarch, were familiar with it, and if we may read a symptomatic meaning into the story of Mary and Martha, then Jesus has likewise, on behalf of women, preferred the desire for a spiritual communality to the desire for serving :

" Mary has chosen the good part; which shall not be taken away from her."

These three types do not in reality emerge so sharply separated nor so plainly defined, nor do they in any

Claassen – types

way exhaust the multiplicity of subjective fetiches. Ria Claassen, premissing her judgments upon certain other signs, has described three other types in one of the most brilliant and—let it be remarked for the benefit of all who deny originality to the female brain—most distinctive contributions to sexual psychology (*Man's Phantom of Woman.—Zürich Discussions, IV.*). These types, according to her, remain eternally the same and repeat themselves in all ages——the phantom of the woman of the Fall; the phantom of the Virgin Mother, and "that most abhorrent that was ever bred in a human brain"—that of the merely sexual woman—"the most convenient object for sultanic lust."

The desire for revenge, the sentimental effusiveness, and the crass meanness which at times accompany the sexual impulse of the man, are brilliantly depicted in these three forms—but all the friendly, tender, comradelike phases, which certainly we cannot ignore as forming part of the relations of the sexes, are ignored by Ria Claassen. For this reason her conception of the sex-relation finds its highest expression in this sombre prognosis : " The Schopenhauerian-Strindbergian phantom, above all, the phantom of the woman of the Fall, is at the same time the oldest and the most modern phantom, the phantom of the future. It is not the greatest possible intimacy between the sexes which is to furnish the solution of future problems, but the greatest possible separateness, at least in the more highly developed specimens."

It is true that we find plenty of indications in modern literature which force us to conclude that the fantastic conceptions of woman as held by the domineering type of man have lost nothing of the ancient sharpness of the sex-antithesis.

But is not the woman-phantom bred from the brain of a John Stuart Mill, a Bebel, Björnsen, or a Walt Whitman, equal in social significance to that of Schopenhauer and Strindberg? And is Goethe, the most consummate representative of amorous genius, no longer to be a prototype for coming generations? It is no doubt due to a misunderstanding—an intentional misunderstanding by means of which German Philistinism seized upon Goethe as its own authority!—that the words, "Betimes let woman learn to serve," meant by him in a general sense, should be interpreted as an expression of Goethe's own attitude towards the feminine sex, notwithstanding the fact that he put these words into the mouth of an heroic girl as an expression of her own voluntary self-resignation—that very Dorothea whom Humboldt accused of being quite unfeminine because in a moment of danger she at once seized weapons—like a man. Goethe's subjective idol is plainly revealed in his view that when woman "is able through sufficient energy to elevate her other advantages she becomes a being than which one could imagine none more perfect. . . . The saying: 'He shall be thy master' is the formula of a barbarous age long since past: men cannot reach the highest degree of cultivation without conceding the same rights to women." His works are ample evidence that he understood how to honour "the heroic greatness of woman with a true manliness."

Must we assume, then, that "woman" is, after all, only a product of the masculine brain, an eternal illusion, a phantom capable of taking all forms without ever possessing a single one?

Woman as an abstraction, as a figment of thought, exists only in the brain of the thinker, and is absolutely dependent upon this—as the nature of thought demands, but woman as an individual exists for herself, and is as noble or as vile, as gifted or as stupid, as weak or as strong, as good or as wicked, as like to man or as unlike him; in short, as diversified as is made necessary by the very nature of the human species. How astonishing that this simple observation, confirmed a thousandfold by life and the representation of life, should only in the rarest cases be able to assert itself against the power of the subjective fetich!

Nothing is of greater importance to women than to battle against the abstractions into which they are constantly being converted by masculine thought. If they wish to achieve power as real persons in the world they must battle against woman as a fetich. That means that they must emerge from their passivity and break the silence that surrounds them, even at the peril of at first producing little that is edifying. There are many men who regard it as the greatest shamelessness or the greatest folly of modern woman that by their confessions and revelations, they should tear the veil which masculine phantasy has woven about them. Silence may have its advantages, but all the advantages in the world will not suffice to compensate a being who has begun to feel herself as a personality—for being taken for something other than she really is.

And even if it is a question of natural predisposition and not of wider knowledge, whether man and woman are to regard each other as free companions or as lord and subject, then it should at least become a question of wider knowledge to fathom the power of the subjective fetich in the relationships of man and woman, and to acknowledge that it is the subjectivity which here remains the unconquerable factor.

VISTAS OF INDIVIDUALITY

In the paintings of the Sistine Chapel, those wonderful revelations of the workings of a great artist's soul, the creation of Adam and Eve is depicted, and also their expulsion from that paradise in which their very natures forbade them to remain. Round about them are the forms of those who would show mankind the road to another paradise, sibyls and prophets, foretellers of the future, teachers and guides towards a higher life. Near them stand the ancestors of Him who shall in time appear as an embodiment of this higher life, fulfilling the hopes deferred for many thousand years, and crowning the steadfast expectation of the faithful.

These pictures represent the most fervent longings of mankind, longings which, in an infinite variety of forms, strive to express themselves, and which have become clearly articulate in the writings of great dreamers, religious and profane. These longings are manifest during the whole history of human thought, in the enthusiastic-ecstatic epochs, and in those of rationalistic positivism. They are the natural yearnings for a higher state of existence, for more perfect conditions, in which an imperfect humanity may advance towards enlightenment and a higher life.

The religious conceptions which at one time appeased

these yearnings with promises of salvation in the next life have now been supplanted by evolutionary ideas. Expectations have been raised of a possible development towards greater and still greater perfection, which, in a happier future, will be the result of the labours of untold generations.

These evolutionary ideas, expressed with almost religious ardour, have found their most perfect exponent in Nietzsche's Zarathustra, who comes to teach the Superman. The present state of mankind appears to him to be one of transition and decline, an arrow of longing directed towards that new and higher form which it will one day reach.

This same desire for a more perfect, more harmonious form of life, free from the senseless incubus of elemental forms, is interwoven with all these sexual problems. For it is in the domain of sex, which binds the permanent characteristics of the individual to the transitory and to the species of which he is a member, that all human strivings towards higher conditions of existence will take place.

The extraordinary interest now taken in this problem —in its lowest manifestations merely an inquisitive plunging into sexual shallows—in its highest an unwearying analysis of all phases of the relations of men towards women—declares itself as a symptom of discordant conditions from which a new order can only be evolved by recognition of the new elements.

In all investigations concerning the male and female we come down to two fundamental questions: what is the meaning and value of individual development, and what should be the aim of such development? The freedom of the individual, the sovereign right of each single person to obey his own inward law, excludes all generalisations having the form of regulations; but social arrangements which are founded on general values, also the impulse towards a more perfect life and a higher development which is most active in the most excellent individuals, shows some objective valuation of sexual characteristics to be necessary.

It may be that the most manly men and the most womanly women are the most perfect representatives of the human species. Although they certainly do not constitute the majority, still, the union of such men and women may produce the greatest possible amount of individual happiness and the most perfect social conditions. If this were so it would be the duty and the ideal of human society to encourage the breeding of this class, and to suppress everything that would interfere with its development. This would necessitate the suppression of all approximation and mingling of sexual characteristics.

To claim that one sex may, in its psychical aspects, be equal to, or even comparable with, the other, is in direct opposition to the conception of a sharply-defined and personal difference in the mentality of the sexes, a difference which is supposed to be the result of historic human development, and to indicate a high stage of culture by the separation of individuals into the two poles of manliness and womanliness. According to this conception, there can be no essential quality of humanness, and since human beings do not exist except as male or female persons, there can be development only along sexual lines. There can be no ideal of a common humanity to which the woman may approach when she develops male characteristics, or the man when he develops female traits. There can be only a male ideal and a female ideal, towards which each individual must strive according to its sex, and from which it must not greatly differ lest it should lose its status and its excellence.

But for all that, abstract " humanity," or " human-ness," does exist as a conception in the thoughts of man, even if not in reality. When we say " the human male," or the " human female," we have used an expression that shows that there is something common to the two which designates the species.

This idea of common traits between the sexes, how-ever sexual separation may dominate actual life, has at all times been recognised as of great importance. If we consider historical development of humanity from this point of view, we shall find that the problem is a very old one, formerly expressed chiefly in religious ideas. But its formulation and accentuation as a feminine problem are quite modern.

Conceptions concerning the nature of the superior human being, and all that tends to raise him to a higher form of life, show a deeply-rooted inclination in human nature to break through the limitations of sex. The sexual differences belong to the lower conditions of existence; in a higher common state we find a com-bination of the two forms of life in operation. When-ever the human mind occupies itself with its relation-ship towards sexuality this view has appeared in many varied forms, both bright and dark.

Wrapped up in mythical symbols and allegories, in the esoteric unapproachability of the Mysteries, this conception of a combination of common elements appears in ancient cults under the hidden significance possessed by hermaphroditism.   In the most ancient representations of the Cypriote Aphrodite as a herma- phrodite idol, we have the coarse material conception of corporeal bi-sexualism.   This, however, is only a naïve expression of the conception of perfection, of the divine nature as an amalgamation of the two sexes in one person.   Other Greek gods also show traces of this con- ception.   Hera gives birth to Hephaestus without the co-operation of Zeus in order to declare her male and female nature; Zeus brings forth Athena from his own head.   This plainly symbolises a mental process as a combination of male and female functions.

Even the spiritualised conception of God handed down by the Jews contains traces of the idea of double sexuality.   In the Hebrew Kabbala the "Sister of the Ancient" appears, under the name Shekinah, as a member of the divine trinity.   One of the conceits of Jewish mysticism defines God as a male being, and the Holy Ghost as a female.   From their sexual union was produced the Son, and with Him the world. (Feuerbach.)

These conceptions are maintained even in Christian thought.   There are indications that the Holy Ghost, who is represented in the form of a dove, was originally the female element in the trinity.   Among the early Christian sects there were some which worshipped the Holy Ghost as a female deity, and even now the Mora- vians call the Holy Ghost the mother of the Saviour. In the religious conceptions that now prevail, the female element has, of course, been excluded from the trinity, but only to take a more especial place as the Immaculate Virgin, the mother of God.

Thus, in this form the old conception of an unsexual or of a supernatural begetting continues. According to this, men of an extraordinarily superior stamp are begotten, not in the usual way, but either by a physical descent of the deity, as in the case of the Greek heroes, or by a virgin mother through the merely spiritual influence of the divinity, as in the legends of Buddha and Christ. For the vanquisher of the ordinary, sexually-limited humanity could not owe his origin to characteristics which bind humanity to a lower life. In one of the later paraphrases of Paracelsus, who calls the sexual organs a " monstrous sign," there occurs the idea that, according to the original plan of creation, the reproduction of human beings should have been, not " salnitric," or after the manner of cattle, but " iliastric," or by magical imagination—in the same way that God created the world out of His own essence.

This " iliastric " being, the original, godlike, perfect man before the Fall, is imagined as bi-sexual. The Jewish mystic recognises an Adam Kadmon, the first Adam, perfect and immortal, who was placed by God in the world as a male and female creature. This is the same conception of the original man that appears among the gnostic sect, the Ophites. Later, as a punishment for his arrogance, the female half was separated from him in the shape of Eve.

Intimately connected with this myth is the well-known story of Aristophanes in Plato's *Symposium*. In this story men are described as having been originally of a dual sex. This condition gave them such strength and ability that in order to diminish their power Zeus cut them in two and made them live as separate halves. Therefore, since every human being is only a part of a former whole, the two portions continually strive to become one again.   Love is the expression of this endeavour to restore the original perfection of human nature.

The idea of such a primitive or mystical union, which has been expanded in the neo-Platonic philosophy, recurs continually in the fantasies of great souls under the influence of love.   Michael Angelo, in his sonnets, speaks of the home-sickness which draws him by means of the eyes of his beloved back to "Eden where we were playmates once."   Goethe, in a poem to Frau von Stein, avers: "Ah! in former ages thou wast my sister or my wife," and Schiller has expressed the same idea in his *Geheimnis der Reminiszenz*, addressed to Laura with all the passionate ardour of his youthful days:

"Waren wir im Strahl erlosch'ner Sonnen schon in Eins zerronnen?
Ja wir waren's! . . .
In innig festverbundnem Wesen waren wir ein Gott . . .
Weine, Laura! Dieser Gott ist nimmer; du und ich des Gottes
schöne Trümmer."

But this digression into the domain of ethereal love, where sexuality is merged with the noblest tendencies of human nature, has no particular purpose beyond proving the fact that these illusions are symptomatic of a special sort of sexual sensitiveness which has its root in the identical conceptions we have been discussing.

This condition of perfection due to the unity of the sexes in primitive ages is closely connected with the transformation from one sex into another.   In the Greek world, standing out above all the rest, are two figures who undergo this transformation.   The seer Tiresias, the superman of prescience, who stands on the boundary line between the human and the divine, transformed himself into a woman, and after nine months changed himself back again from a woman into a man. Hercules, the superman of action, who had traversed the whole cycle of human labour, was in his relations with Omphale a symbol of the same idea, although, indeed, in this case the actual treatment of it is very commonplace.

To this category also belong those orgiastic festivals of ancient civilisations in which men and women exchanged their clothes, a symbolic action having the esoteric significance that the sexes may, through this exchange, attain to a higher stage of life. In order to be able to penetrate into the deepest mysteries of life, the male must accept something from the female; he must have a desire to overcome the limitation of sex and abandon the ordinary views of the profane multitude, that is to say, the belief in an absolute and indivisible development of masculinity.

The energetic barbaric expression of this desire was the rite of mutilation which the priests of Cybele underwent. After that operation they were also obliged, in order to rid themselves of all male characteristics, to shave off their beards and to wear women's clothes. The idea that it is necessary for a man seeking the higher life to abandon all the outward signs of sex still finds an echo in that catholic custom which prescribes that priests shall not wear beards and shall wear the dress assigned to females—a cassock reaching to the feet. When the apostle Paul speaks of those who " made themselves eunuchs for the Kingdom of Heaven's sake," the allusion to the ancient rite and its application to the new doctrines are unmistakable.

Conceptions which in the ancient world were concealed beneath the mysteries of various cults were brought by Christianity into the light of day, and made accessible to all mankind as a new ideal of life. Never have the renunciation and the suppression of sexuality been more strongly, more comprehensively, or more convincingly advocated than by the upholders of this new ideal. The Pauline saying, " Here is neither Jew nor Greek, neither bond nor free, neither male nor female, but ye are all one in Jesus Christ," shows most clearly that Christianity embraced all humanity without distinction of race, rank, or sex. As long as its attitude towards worldly affairs was consistent, Christianity recognised no distinction between the two sexes as to their moral worth, for it expected its followers to be far above all sexuality. Manliness and womanliness came not within the ken of this view of life.

If, however, we accept Hartpole Lecky's view that the transition from the ancient to the Christian ideal of life was a transition from the male to the female ideal, then we must admit that the male had to give up all that was specifically masculine in his nature. The sex virtues are entirely absent from the spiritual characteristics of the saints; both sexes are alike in their manner of life and thought. Fine qualities of specifically sexual character belong only to secular or lower life; the fact that Christian precepts were not always based on the supposition that in the Christian community there were neither male nor female, is only a sign of that divergence between theory and practice which is common to all human endeavour.

Apart from religious conceptions and ascetic renunciation of sex, there are other symptoms that point to a striving towards unity independent of sex. Christianity sought to raise mankind to a higher plane by grafting female traits into the male nature; the Renaissance in which so many ancient elements come again to life, set up the masculine type as a pattern for women. It was considered a distinction for a woman to have mental excellences similar to those possessed by men. At that period the woman of good position had to strive in the same way as a man towards attaining a definite personality, complete in every respect. The same condition of heart and mind that made a man perfect was also supposed to make a woman perfect, . . . we have only to notice the thoroughly masculine bearing of the women in the legends of the heroes, and in the compositions of Bojardo and Ariosto, to recognise that there is a definite ideal in all of them." (Burckhardt, *Civilisation in the Renaissance Period*.) It was considered as the noblest bond between man and woman "if their hearts were fired with the same feelings, their bodies animated with the same glowing soul, so that each should have an equal impulse towards a higher life, . . . and each should choose the other as lord and master."

These are the words of that man, gifted with a lofty prophetic soul, who created the Jesus-Apollo, the god of a renovated world, the superhuman compound of two great culture epochs. Michael Angelo did not set his Messiah " on the right hand of God," as Christian tradition had done, in order that as an immortal judge he might choose the righteous and reject the wicked; no, at his side appears the woman who, with the compassion born of perfect understanding, bends mercifully not only towards the saved but also towards the damned.

The Christian, like the Renaissance ideal, was realised only in a few individuals, the highest examples of

humanity. But if we search for the traces of this ideal
in literature we shall find that it is not altogether lost.
It is strikingly evident in that glorious period from the
end of the eighteenth to the middle of the nineteenth
century. Many of Goethe's phrases are based on this
ideal of sexual unity. He declared that woman could
profitably acquire certain masculine qualities, " for if she
could add energy to her other excellences, she would
form the most perfect being that could be imagined."
To Julia he addressed these words: " With happy skill
thou dost unite a manlike strength to woman's tenderness." Finally, we may recall that esoteric phrase, so
full of meaning and so little understood, " the eternal
feminine draws us onward."

Then there is that strange creation Mignon. Goethe
himself, in his conversations with the Chancellor von
Müller, says that the whole romance was written for her
sake, and that underlying all of the other characters there
is a strain of something more noble and more universal. It is impossible to mistake the artistic intention
of creating a being whose soul was unburdened by sex.
The fine poetic glamour that surrounds this figure
belongs partly to the child, the sexless being of reality,
partly to the angel, the sexless being of the imagination.
" Let me but seem to be till I may be . . . and those
heavenly forms no question make of woman or of man."

Balzac's Seraphita is related to Mignon, but has a
more evident intention of showing the mystical combination of male and female qualities. She is a being
far excelling the ordinary run of mortals: she is of lofty
spiritual origin, to the maiden who loves her she appears
a perfect man, in the eyes of the man who loves her she
is a perfect woman. There is a strong personal interest

in the history of the evolution of this character, because
Balzac created it to please the woman whom he loved,
and, as he says in his dedication, "in the form dreamed
of by you and by me, too, when I was still a child."

The men of that epoch have thought more freely
and more deeply over the sex question than the men of
the present day. Chateaubriand, in his *Memoirs*, makes
this admission, so seldom made by men, that if he had
had his choice he would have created himself as a woman
on account of his preference for women. Gentz, in a
letter to Rahel Varnhagen, wrote quite frankly: "Do
you know, my dear one, why our intercourse has become
so perfect? I will tell you. You are an infinitely productive being while I am infinitely receptive. You are a
great man, and I am the first of all the women that have
ever lived."

It sounds like a commentary on that famous passage
at the end of *Faust* when we read in Daumer's *Religion
of the New Age*: "The submission of human beings
to what is natural, the submission of the male to
the female is . . . the highest and, indeed, the only
virtue and holiness that can exist." In his *Confidential
Letters*, Schleiermacher expresses similar ideas about
Schlegel's *Lucinde*: "At last the true and heavenly
Venus has been discovered, . . . a being of the deepest
and holiest feelings, created by merging and uniting the
two halves of humanity into one mystic whole. Those
whose eyes cannot thus pierce into divinity and into
humanity and cannot comprehend the mysteries of this
religion, are not worthy to be citizens of the new world."

In the same strain he has composed his *Catechism
of Reason for Noble Women*, in which he writes: "I
believe in the infinite humanity which existed before it

assumed the cloak of the masculine and the feminine.
. . . I believe in the power of will and of cultivation to
bring me back into the infinite, . . . and to make me
independent of the bonds of sex."

Lucinde itself, that worthy, earnest, virtuous work,
as Schleiermacher calls it, contains passages in which
the suspension of sexual antithesis is highly praised.
Thus, Friedrich Schlegel calls the exchanging of the
parts in the play of love "a wonderfully intelligent
allegory of the perfecting of the male and female into
one entire human." When he describes "the permanent feeling of harmonious warmth" as the highest
stage of love, he declares that, "When a youth
feels thus he loves no longer as a mere man, but at the
same time also as a woman. In him is humanity perfected, and he has climbed to the very highest summit
of life."

Human personality becomes hermaphrodite not only
as a result of overpowering love causing a mingling of
two beings and an "exchange of souls," but also
through that great preponderation of intellect which is
produced by living in the domain of the higher culture.
According to Schopenhauer's interpretation of the world,
in which he makes the will the primary or male, the
intellect the secondary or female principle, man in his
intellectual characteristics must be a male-female being
produced by the union of these two principles in one
individual; a deduction which, however, was not actually
reached by Schopenhauer himself. We need not lay
much stress on this arbitrary and metaphysical indication of man's natural inclination towards sex analogies.

The contemplative condition produced by continual

intellectual occupation also causes an approximation of the male to the female character. Nietzsche, who otherwise was an advocate of extreme sex-differentiation, repeatedly points out the similarity to a woman produced in a man by mental pregnancy, an analogy of which he is so fond that he has employed it with several variations.

It is a matter of common observation that the man of genius does not show the psychic characters of extreme sex differentiation, but in many ways approximates to the female, and even to the child. Perhaps this is on account of his greater irritability—which is considered as a peculiarity of the feminine sex—owing to which external stimulations act more swiftly and more strongly upon him than upon the ordinary run of men. The intensity of these external impressions, together with the energy of the impulses from within, produces that unreliable temperament manifested in men of genius as an unaccountable and uncontrollable changeability of mood —which is likewise supposed to be a special characteristic of the feminine sex.

That well-known symptom of feminine sensitiveness, a predisposition towards weeping, is also shared by men of genius. Goethe, for instance, was easily moved to tears. It was also Goethe who recognised in himself a peculiarity which is specially female, receptivity; that is to say, a power of vitally assimilating strange and alien things. Unless it possess a receptivity beyond the ordinary measure of mankind, genius cannot continue its existence, receptivity is quite as necessary to it as that productivity which is generally considered as its most essential feature. Genius is not to be regarded as an augmentation of the specifically male nature, but as an expansion beyond the limitations of individual sex differentiation. It is a synthesis of the male and female nature which is also exemplified in women of genius, who likewise show no extreme sex differentiation, but more often approximate to the male type.

In the relationship between the conscious and the unconscious life, genius also appears as a synthesis. Ricarda Huch mentions it in her book upon the golden age of romance. The men who act, as it were, unconsciously, she classes as the male type, those who have perception, and, being conscious of it, cannot transmute it into action, she classes as the artistic or female type; genius, she thinks, unites the two qualities, and is both male and female. As a corollary of this deduction, she considers that the harmoniously constituted " men of the future " will have an hermaphrodite character.

The most striking example of how manifestly mental productivity can assume the character of hermaphroditism, is afforded by the conceptions of men of genius which Richard Wagner expressed when discussing the connection between poetry and music. He himself, being a poet as well as a musician, considered musical composition as a female function. "Music is a woman," and cannot be fruitful unless impregnated by the male word. Boldly and profoundly he has elaborated this idea in his *Opera and Drama*. His views about specific sexuality are shown by such sentences as, " The truly female is only to be thought of as the highest form of love's longing, whether manifested in a man or in a woman "; or, " The connection between intelligence and feeling is purely human, and is distinctive of the human race. Both the female and the male are sustained by what is purely human; they do not become human until

united in the bonds of love." Therefore, he did not
hesitate to ascribe the excellence of the music of
Mozart's *Don Juan* to the fact that here " the composer
is shown by the character of his music to have had the
nature of a loving woman "; and the greatness of
Beethoven, who felt the necessity of seeking the help
of a poet for his principal works, he ascribes to his
having become " an entire, that is to say, a complete,
human being, subject to the conditions both of the male
and of the female."

It is not the objective meaning of these sentences in
their aspect as theories about music, but the subjective
and symptomatic significance—the conception that a
perfect human being must be subject to the conditions
both of the male and of the female, that comes into
consideration here. Emerson also expresses the same
idea when he says, " In the brain there are both male
and female qualities, . . . in the mental world we practically change our sex every moment." This is his
commentary on the ideas of Swedenborg, that mysterious spirit so difficult to understand, under whose
influence Balzac wrote his romance *Seraphita*. Strindberg—in every way a man whose nature was decidedly
masculine—rose to such a pitch as to say, " For a man
to love a child it is necessary that he should put away
his masculinity and become a woman and love with the
sexless love of the angels, as Swedenborg calls it."

It would be a great mistake to regard the views expressed in these passages, which have been culled at
random and do not represent all that has been said in
this strain, as merely a symptom of a pathological variation from normal sexuality. They are the expression of

views which lead us into the highest mental planes, they are the conceptions of the noblest and most distinguished men of their time; they are ideas which come to the front much more decidedly in the golden age of culture than in periods of decline. Those I have quoted refer exclusively to mental conditions described either literally or else symbolically. There is no allusion to any latent bodily bi-sexuality. No one can doubt that physiologically the course of evolution towards homologous monosexuality," towards definite sex-differentiation in the individual, constitutes the most desirable tendency. Every deviation from the normal physiological sex characteristics renders the individual an imperfect being; bodily hybridism is repulsive because it indicates incompleteness, a defective and faulty structure. A human being cannot possess real health and beauty unless the body is perfect sexually as well as in every other respect. It must not, however, be forgotten that both sexes have been developed from an originally hermaphrodite organism, and traces of this double sexuality will be found in each. According to the latest biological theories, it seems probable that traces of double sexuality will be found to be permanent in all the more highly organised beings.

While it is an advantage that modern thought, regarding all problems by the light of natural science, and not merely from the moral point of view, has considered mental phenomena as processes of nature, yet it is a great defect that it has no standards of comparison except those of the majority, of the average. From the point of view of natural science, the average is to be taken as the normal, and it regards every deviation from this as a symptom of disease or degeneration.

[handwritten marginalia: mental, but NOT bodily hermaphrodism!]

This confusion between the normal based on the average, and the normal based on the best specimens of the species, deprives scientific conceptions of a proper standard for estimating the highest and most uncommon individuals of the human race.   According to these conceptions, the average man is the exclusive type of what is sound and healthy, therefore the man who is far above the average is necessarily classed as an abnormality.   No consideration is given to the fact that such a man bears the signs and presages of a higher development, things which, from the evolutionary point of view, are of the greatest value.   These signs ought not to be considered as pathological, because genius betokens greater functional activity, while a pathological state lowers this activity.

This habit of considering the average man is the cause of the smug dead-level and dreariness of modern mental life.   The highest and best examples are put on one side as factors in the life of the community, and ordinary, every-day people are given a higher place than they deserve.   In the horrible "levelled-down-to-the-average" culture of the present day the average man, equipped with a theoretically developed intelligence, is the predominating factor, and he regards himself as the proper pattern for the rest.   But the standard of Fantasy, of Impulsiveness, of Introspection, or of any other quality characteristic of individuality which is now considered normal, is not the same as it was a hundred years ago, and possibly it will again be different even in the coming generation.   .

If we look upon human thought as one of the processes of nature, we must also consider the various views on sexuality as symptoms of the various forces working in the race. These views are so opposed, and recur so constantly, dividing the individuals of each sex into groups, that we may suppose two opposing tendencies to be working in the evolution of the human race. One is directed towards the preservation of the race character common to both sexes, while the other tends towards the teleological differentiation of each. One strives for a human type irrespective of male or female, strengthening the characteristics of the race common to both sexes, the other tries to produce extremes of sexuality and requires differentiation for the sake of reproduction and transmission.

In these two tendencies we see the opposing fundamental forces which maintain the equilibrium of nature. The individuals in whom the centripetal tendency of the race is predominant are inclined to attach most importance to the characteristics common to the two sexes, and to consider sex-differences as secondary and subordinate, or even to disregard them. Individuals with centrifugal tendencies consider sexual contrast as a cardinal point in moral development, and hold every approximation to the common human type to be an aberration or degeneration.

From the purely contemplative standpoint, each tendency seems natural, and the struggle between them appears as a necessary condition for development. However, as soon as we cease to be mere " seekers after knowledge," and begin to act and to exercise our judgment as members of this human race, we are obliged in the course of nature to play the part assigned to us by our own fundamental qualities. Our impartiality cannot extend farther than a theoretical recognition of the inevitability of the struggle. Even if we confess that our views are merely subjective, we are still obliged to regulate our life and actions according to these subjective views.

Therefore, the ideas about the results likely to be produced by continual development in the two sexes will differ considerably in different individuals. The influence of civilisation, which especially tends to produce a greater and accentuated diversity in individual life, includes the possibility of evolution towards the extremes of sexuality, as well as that of approximation of the two types. In accordance with their individual natures, civilised people are either more closely related or more widely separated in their sexuality than are races of savages. This would give support to both theories, and might prove that the result of human evolution will be a differentiation towards the opposite poles of sexuality, or that it will be an approximation towards a common human type.

That these tendencies should be more active in the mental life of the present day than ever before is perhaps due to the equilibrium in the relations between the sexes having been disturbed by a temporary preponderance of the centrifugal tendency. There is some danger of this disturbance causing a hypertrophy of the intellectual life on the one side, and of the emotional life on the other. This divergence in the character of the two sexes would in time diminish or prevent all intercourse between them.

If we try to distinguish the various types of individuals according to their psychosexual qualities, and according to the degree in which these opposing tendencies are manifested, we find three types, the upholders of three different ideals with regard to sexual differences.

The commonest type is the _acratic,_ the partially developed being of unmitigated sexuality whose whole personality is determined by teleological sex characteristics. All the hackneyed declarations as to what the " wholly male " and the " truly female " should be, and do, are the utterances of these acratic people. In examples of this type, patterns of the most manly man and of the most womanly woman, centrifugal sexuality finds its best exponents. Carried to its extremes, this acratic tendency produces licentious domineering masculinity and weak, insignificant and passive, or else crafty, false and ludicrous femininity, forms of sex-differentiation which are the complements of each other and equal in nature and in origin.

Just as acratic persons are part and parcel of the every-day reality of life, so do we find *iliastric* persons, the highest type of centripetal sexuality, citizens, one might say, of another world and strangers to this earth. They have overcome sex, and through this victory have become endowed with higher supersensual powers. The most perfect representatives of *iliastric* humanity in western civilisation are the Christian saints, for in their mental and moral characteristics all sexual differentiation has been thoroughly eliminated.

During the greater part of the history of man's mental development we find signs of an unwearying struggle to rise above and beyond specific sexuality in order to attain a higher condition of existence; in the early days of ancient civilisation we find it in the priestly ideals, then in the Indian Yoga doctrines, and in those ideas which gave rise to the knighthood of the Holy Grail.

It is especially characteristic of Christianity and of Buddhism, both of which regard the iliastric, sexless condition as a preliminary stage towards the attainment of the kingdom of heaven or of Nirvana, a kingdom not of this world but of a world of peace reposing in infinite perfection, in contradistinction to the world of creation in which the centrifugal force of movement rages in everlasting strife.

The importance that we are to attach to this most extreme expression of centripetal tendency must ultimately depend on our religious beliefs, or at least on our general outlook upon life. It may be questioned whether the longing for another, more perfect form of life than that conditioned by sexuality, the longing for an all-embracing oneness, for undisturbed repose, be merely a symptom of an infirmity of will or a manifestation of a higher principle leading us on beyond the ordinary world of corporeal sensation. When this longing takes the form of an asceticism hostile to life, of a renunciation whose chief law is the " mortifying of the flesh," and particularly of sex, it must appear repugnant to that view of life which attaches most importance to existence in this world and excludes speculations about the possibility of any future life. For beliefs that are founded upon conditions not applicable to this present life must seem unjustifiable to those who take that view.

The ascetic principle, therefore, cannot raise the higher man entirely above sex, because he does not represent a preliminary stage for a metaphysical existence free from sexuality, but a perfecting of what is attainable to humanity in a form of life bound body and soul to the earth. The representatives of higher humanity in a monistic sense will be those whose psychophysical

constitution enables them to overstep the bounds of
sexuality, and to raise and increase the inward relationships between the sexes—those beings who are subject
to the conditions both of the male and of the female—
synthetic man.

The most favourable condition for a harmonious
development of personality is not an extreme, but a
qualified, sexuality. In such a personality there will be
an equilibrium of the two opposing tendencies, the
centrifugal which seeks sexual differentiation for every
individual, and the centripetal which maintains the
common characteristics of the race. Qualified sexuality
is produced by all cultural influences which bring the
sexes nearer together and facilitate an interchange
between them; such influences are favourable to the
synthetic existence and the ideals of life which arise
from it.

The standard of his value as a psychosexual individuality each man must estimate for himself, since it
is quite relative in so far as it regards his personal
destiny. For in this respect each person's life can be
gauged only by reference to his relation to some individual of the other sex who may be adequate for him.
For in their relations to each other their happiness
depends not so much on the quantity, plus or minus, of
the manliness or womanliness of each, as on the equivalents which they can offer each other. Therefore we
must not estimate single individuals according to their
degree of manliness or womanliness, but according to
the equivalents their natures afford.

The sex relationships of acratic persons may also be
subjectively very happy. The man who possesses the
concomitants of his domineering sexual nature will give

as much happiness to his submissive and dependent wife
as is possible for such people, if by virtue of his
domineering habits he is able to be her protector, supporter, and defender. It is not the one-sidedness of
sex-differentiation which is primarily the source of
happiness or unhappiness for individuals. Unhappiness
is produced by a deficiency of the concomitants in
dyscratic natures, those natures in which the synthesis
is not fully perfected, so that they have some of the
tendencies of the acratic type and some of the synthetic.
A woman who by her erotic disposition is bound to be
submissive and subjugated, and yet otherwise is desirous
of having a freely personal life, or a man who must be
a sexual dictator to a woman without having that personal energy which also gives power outside the sexual
sphere—both of these, by reason of the dyscrasy of their
nature, will be unable to live in harmonious relations
with a member of the other sex or to find sexual
equilibrium.

Except for the individual, these estimates concerning
happiness are not of much value; but, considered objec-
tively, the enrichment and broadening of the individual
life which result from the amalgamation of two people
of different sex is of immense advantage. The synthetic
being is, in this respect, superior to the acratic, just as
the man who can see is superior to the blind man,
although the latter may not be aware of his inferiority,
and may, under certain circumstances, even lead a
happier life.

Acratic and synthetic persons have utterly different
ideas about love. You have only to listen to what the
most manly and the most womanly think of one another, or to the descriptions which they give of love.

They do not strive for complete agreement, for unlimited devotion, for mutual and unreserved confidence;
in short, for those relations which in western civilisation
have attained a lofty place in our ideals of social
morality. That type of sexual relationship that Car-
penter describes in his book, *Love's Coming of Age*,
a book full of the spirit of synthetic humanity, is not at
all suitable for acratic people.

The distinguishing mark of synthetic people is that
they have an outlook over the barriers of sex, a power
of sweeping away the bonds entailed by sexuality,
enabling them to reach a mental sphere common to both
sexes of the human species. The wider the sphere the
more easily will the process of amalgamation be carried
out, the more extensive and perfect will it be. Since
sex does not connote for synthetic people an entirely
different sort of existence, but only a different form of
being, they are able, apart from sexual affairs, to enjoy
a common existence. Thus, they raise themselves to a
universality of perception which is denied to the acratic.
Their nature acquires an element of freedom which
enables individuals of even moderate talents to have a
liberal and intelligent understanding of the other sex,
while those who are not synthetic in nature cannot break
through the barriers of their sex, even though their
minds may be of the most emancipated type.

That type of existence which represents the most
extreme sex-differentiation, and assigns to the male
absolute activity, and to the female absolute passivity—
though, indeed, this is only an imaginary conception,
and hardly likely to be met with in reality—would exclude its participants from all comprehension of the other
sex, and debar them from all mental fellowship in their
sexual alliances. In short, we may assume that a man

can only understand a woman's nature in the same proportion in which he possesses this nature within himself, and the same statement will also hold good for a woman. The words man and woman are to be taken in their proper esoteric sense as symbols of forces which are manifested, more or less strongly, in the inner life of actual individuals of different sexes, taking the physiological analogy of receptive and negative for the feminine force, creative and positive for the masculine.

Only for acratic beings does sexuality at the same time connote onesidedness ; the synthetic will find that sexuality is the very condition which enables them to emerge from their own limited individual existence and to enter into a life subject to other physical conditions. To them the life of the other sex does not appear as something strange and unaccountable, but as something closely related, originally a part of their own life and now the complement of their special individual existence advancing to meet them from without.

It is true that acratic persons seek in individuals of the other sex the complement of their own natures, but as they have little or no common ground of fellowship it is only in their opposites that they may render their natures more complete. The assumption that the greatest contrasts exert the greatest attraction for one another is based on insufficient observation, and is only true of the acratic. The erotic attraction between the synthetic is a much more complicated phenomenon, and far more difficult to analyse than the attraction between the acratic who, being. uncompounded, are therefore more primitive and simple. The determining factors are not the number and quantity of contrasts, but the particular sort that are required to render the individual

more complete. A synthetic woman will find no personal attraction in an acratic man, although in him the
psychical sexual contrast is infinitely greater than in the
synthetic man, who alone is able to satisfy her deepest
feelings; nor, *vice-versâ*, can the synthetic man satisfy
the acratic woman.

We may conceive this sex-differentiation as the result
of a progressive movement which might be represented
as the path described by the swinging of a pendulum.
The principle of unity, which is the basis on which the
human race exists as a species, might be pictured as the
moving pendulum, and the mutual attraction which is
determined by the individual sex-differentiation might
be imagined as the acting force. Between the two extreme points, equi-distant from the centre, the pendulum
swings to and fro. Each point in its arc of oscillation
has a corresponding point on the other side of the
median line, and at an equal distance from it. The
extreme points of the arc have the greatest distance from
one another, while towards the middle the distances
between the corresponding points grow less. The most
remarkable positions of the moving pendulum are the
two extreme points, which show the limits of the path
and also its greatest contrasts, and the middle, which
represents a state of rest. In between lie innumerable
points of a corresponding equilibrium. Inasmuch as
these symmetrically arranged points correspond to one
another, and we regard one-half of the path as the
domain of male sex-differentiation, and the other as
the female, then the various sex individualities will be
seen to correspond to one another and find their expression in the attraction that they mutually exert.

Iliastric humanity represents the middle state of rest,

the acratic in its most absolute form represents the extreme ends of the swing. The points between the middle and the end may be classed as inner or outer, according to the amount of their distance from the middle point. The nearer the middle the greater the relationship, the farther from it the greater the contrast of the sexes. The outer group towards the ends of the path belong to the domain of acratic humanity, the inner towards the middle comprise the synthetic. In this illustration it is plainly seen why, excluding all superficial appearances, there is a great contrast not only between the two extremes of the sexes but also why the groups near the middle are so far removed from those of their own sex at the very end points that the similarity of their physiological nature affords no bond of fellowship or of comprehension between them. What seems incomprehensible and contradictory in this sex-differentiation, and in its relation to individual differentiation, as long as we look upon the terms " man " and " woman " as absolutely binding definitions, becomes clear and natural so soon as we have obtained an insight into the complexity of psychosexual phenomena and their relations to one another.

Those who look upon sex-modification as a secondary phenomenon, and consider the typical sex peculiarities of human nature only as the teleological conditions of the sexual relations of the sexes to each other—conditions which will have more or less influence on each individual according to his mental constitution—will acknowledge that a belief in innumerable gradations in the psychical nature of the two sexes may give a better grasp of the meaning of individuality and of its importance to human society.

These gradations do not mean (as Weiniger thought) that the approximation of the manly to the womanly necessitates the man being less manly or the woman less womanly. They have nothing to do with the feminine man nor with the masculine woman, those two results of degeneration in the spheres of centrifugal sexuality. The womanish man has a lower sort of manliness, because the base female peculiarities which characterise him are considered as defects even in a woman. The synthetic man, however, does not become lower through his compound nature, he loses nothing; he gains. The approximation towards unity carries him beyond sex towards what is neither male nor female, but purely human.

The higher life, the life in the domain of intellect, requires that the personality shall possess qualities which transcend the limitations of the merely primitive life. These qualities are not differentiated sexually, for the simple reason that they have not been acquired by evolution for the benefit nor the purposes of sex. Their origin is rather to be sought for in religious strivings in which the highest aim was the overcoming of sexuality.

The ascetic renunciation of sex is intimately connected with the metaphysical aspirations which have such high importance in the history of human mental progress. This association has been taken as a sign that these aspirations are a symptom of the weakening and decay of the elementary impulses of life. But is it not possible that this association may be interpreted in quite a different way? If all manifestations of consciousness are to be taken as physiological processes in the brain, then the mental history of mankind must be the history of the increasing independence of the brain.

The conception formed by those who hold dualistic views of human existence, that sex is an attribute only of the body, the inferior and perishable part of the human being, while the superior and immortal part is sexless and the nearer perfection the more it frees itself from the claims of sex, suggests a special physiological process of evolution for the human organism. Perhaps this dualistic conception is only an expression of the dualism of the physiological constitution which makes the brain a second and relatively independent organism existing in the body. The strange delusion that bodies are inhabited by a higher being, an immortal and sexless soul, is perhaps a conscious reflection of a physical process, just as in dream-life one can often see the erstwhile conditions of the organism appear within the consciousness symbolised and fantastically modified. Do we not have a similar experience with the illusion of free will which is so incompatible with the results obtained by a study of the human understanding? Yet this illusion is regarded as an absolute certainty by many people, especially by those who have brought their sexual impulses under the control of their will-power. Is not the whole history of human morality, in which the controlling and overcoming of sexuality occupies so large a space, fundamentally nothing but this struggle of the brain for independence?

Let us leave metaphysical paraphrases. The development of the control of certain centres of consciousness by other centres, the existence of a precedence among them which indicates a submission of the lower centres to the guidance of the higher, is a necessary condition for all mental culture. It represents a most valuable acquirement when it is the cause of those inner conflicts

and resistances which alienate intellectual men from their
primitive nature.

The underlying cause of this battling against sex is
not the repulsiveness and sinfulness of sexuality, as those
people who sought to free themselves from its dominion
were wont to believe.   Retrospectively, this battle
appears as a fierce evolutionary struggle of humanity to
surmount the teleological barriers of sex in order to
obtain facilities for reaching a higher mental plane.
The autonomy of the brain which has been acquired by
this long and weary struggle is permanent, although the
illusions which were begotten during its continuance
have now vanished.   From this autonomy other ideals
will arise which will open new perspectives in human
life, will give it that brilliancy and warmth and that
joyfully impulsive force which always accompany the
birth of new ideals.

No longer can the lives of those who have risen
above the average be entirely occupied with a struggle
against sex and with combating the claims made by the
race on the individual.   The reconciliation between
race and personality on a higher plane of perception takes
the place of "the mortifying of the flesh," that moral
ideal of a bygone epoch in the development of mankind.
But this reconciliation is only possible when sex no
longer acts in any way as a fetter on personality, either
in the form of uncontrollable impulses or in the form
of teleological limitations working from within or from
without.

For lofty souls nothing is more unbearable than the
idea of bondage to sex.   To be excluded on account of
sex from any possibility of development, from any
road to knowledge within the realm of human exist-

Sex as essential, but goal: to overcome sex!

ence, can but awaken in such souls a hatred against sex. It is they who eagerly reach towards those conditions and habits of life by which synthetic ideas may be promoted and strengthened, for their self-consciousness does not rest on the qualities which are typical of their sex, but on those which lead them beyond their sex.

Wonderful and indeed awe-inspiring is the operation in certain individualities of those characteristics which tend to abolish their primitive sexual nature because it is contradictory to their ideals. For this reason firm and intrepid self-reliance, advancing with initiative, inflexibility, and strength of will, is more to be esteemed in a woman than in a man. For these qualities in a man betoken only a conversion of sex teleology into a higher sphere of mental life, but in a woman they show an overstepping of the bounds set by teleological conditions for the ordinary female individual. That is the real gist of the following sentence of Grillparzer's: " The noble woman is partially, nay, wholly, masculine, only her failings make her feminine."

Nature has given the male the great advantage of allowing his teleological sex conditions to produce those qualities which are favourable to the development of free personality, while the female must first overcome her teleological nature before she can develop such qualities. But specific sex is a barrier even for a man, because it excludes him from comprehending the other half of mankind, and thus restricts him. Free in the highest sense—more so than the " wholly masculine " can ever be—will be that man who possesses sufficient synthetic force to attain by assimilation a higher and more comprehensive state of being. This force, which is wanting in the acratic man since it is not compatible with his teleological sex nature, is nothing else than a capacity for self-sacrifice. Sacrifice, the only means by which the lonely "ego" confined within the limits of his own being, like a prisoner in an isolation cell, may escape and associate with the most precious thing the world can produce—a human soul!

If we trace the lines of the past which lead forward into the future, we find in unmistakable outlines the ideal of a humanity in which sex has a better and happier significance than it has hitherto possessed. Those moral strivings of personality to break the bonds of sex which attained their climax in the renunciation of a world based on the idea of creation, are now directed towards another form of life in which there is a possibility of overcoming the bonds of sex without renunciation. None but synthetic human beings can be the creators of this form of life. But it cannot be done by men alone, without the aid of women. Unless women work with men on a footing of equality, this ideal cannot be realised. The contribution which woman can make to human culture by reason of the path she has had to follow in the course of her evolution, is necessary for the completion of man's work. It is to the honour of the female sex that it is especially the women who, in the mental culture of the day, represent the ideal of unity, and in this there is a guarantee that women will help to realise it.

This ideal is not novel, it is not a discovery that will have to be made by some future generation, although every generation must make it for itself. It is not a levelling, constraining rule of a definite manner of existence, but a living form of freedom for the individuality which springs eternally from the breast of

Nature, an inexhaustible source of new possibilities of evolution and new forms of being.

Happy is he who in his individuality possesses an instrument on which the world may play in all its wonderful fulness. Sexuality will be for him a means by which he may seize upon the very heart of life, its deepest sorrows and its most entrancing joys, its most dreadful abysses and its most radiant heights.